REINVENTING PRACTICE IN A DISENCHANTED WORLD

REINVENTING PRACTICE IN A DISENCHANTED WORLD

Bourdieu and Urban Poverty in Oaxaca, Mexico

CHELEEN ANN-CATHERINE MAHAR

UNIVERSITY OF TEXAS PRESS *Austin*

Requests for permission to reproduce material from this work should be sent to:
Permissions
University of Texas Press
P.O. Box 7819
Austin, TX 78713–7819
www.utexas.edu/utpress/about/bpermission.html

⊗ The paper used in this book meets the minimum requirements of
ANSI/NISO Z39.48-1992 (R1997) (Permanence of Paper).

LIBRARY OF CONGRESS CATALOGING-IN-PUBLICATION DATA

Mahar, Cheleen.
Reinventing practice in a disenchanted world : Bourdieu and urban
poverty in Oaxaca, Mexico / Cheleen Ann-Catherine Mahar.
        p.   cm.
Includes bibliographical references and index.
ISBN 978-0-292-72192-0 (cloth : alk. paper)
1. Urban poor—Mexico—Oaxaca (State)—Case studies.   2. Oaxaca
(Mexico : State)—Social conditions—Case studies.   3. Bourdieu, Pierre,
1930–2002.   4. Sociology—Methodology.   I. Title.
HV4051.A60295   2009
305.5'69097274091732—dc22
2009041711

FOR CHRISTOPHER

CONTENTS

As a young woman in graduate school, I went with other anthropologists to work with the urban poor in Oaxaca, Mexico. Since then, over a period of thirty years, a group of Mexican women, as well as a number of their daughters and sons, have confided stories about their lives to me. These stories tell of the struggles they overcame to create homes in a squatter settlement on an urban hillside, on land they did not own. Here they raised their families, found work, and created a future for themselves. Between 1968 and 1974, I worked with another anthropologist in Colonia Hermosa. Later, from 1996 to 2000, I returned again to visit and to exchange news and stories.

These accounts were private, yet the inhabitants of Colonia Hermosa have allowed me to share them more widely in order to explicate the broader story of Mexico and globalization. The people I spoke to, and who became friends, felt their experiences might be helpful to others following a similar path. In general, these were rural people coming to the city for the first time, and they believed their own journeys might serve as useful sources of information for others. The relationships I developed in this community were based on trust: trust that I would not misrepresent their stories, and trust that I would not use their names. I have taken pains in transcribing their words, as the process of writing clearly changes the experience of the actual interview. I have tried to set each individual in context, and to draw a vivid picture both of the circumstances of each interview session and of each person's broader life history.

Subjectivity is essential to the story social science tells, but like its counterpart, objectivity, it is rarely enough. Our job in anthropology and sociology is not only to record and witness the lives of others, but also to learn how to listen at a deeper level and, through listening, discern the social logic of the domination and symbolic violence that are common in the global community. The personal accounts presented in this book are, on one hand, personal and subjective, but on the other, reflective of larger societal structures. In Colonia Hermosa, families and individuals are framed by personal dispositions and familial logic, but also by a larger social logic of late and developing capitalism. My hope is that readers will find that this book helps unlock both the logic of the self and, in part, the logic of the global system. The theoretical armature of the analysis is taken from the work of Pierre Bourdieu and offers a very specific interpretation of the daily life of the urban poor within the context of a developing economy in Mexico.

I also hope that students will find this book of value as an introduction to ethnography. It should be of use to those who are interested in the lives of the urban poor, and who want to approach the task of ethnographic fieldwork. Just as I undertook this study as a graduate student first entering the field, it is my hope that the text that follows will be helpful in guiding other ethnographers through their first forays into practical anthropology.

ACKNOWLEDGMENTS

Over the course of my fieldwork and the writing of this book, many people have been generous with their help. First and foremost, I am grateful for the life of Pierre Bourdieu, who, long before he died, helped and encouraged me in this project, and spent many hours with me making sure that I understood his sociology. His work has changed the entire field of social theory in Europe and the United States. What many readers perhaps do not realize is that he was a kind, mentoring person with regard to his younger students and colleagues. His heart was full.

I am particularly indebted to my friends, compadres, and informants from Colonia Hermosa who continued over the years to give of their time, information, and ideas so that I might complete my project. I also want to thank those anthropologists who worked with me in Oaxaca many years ago, and those who welcomed me back to Oaxaca in the late 1990s: Michael Higgins, the late Cecil Welte, Arthur Murphy, and Martha Rees.

I would especially like to thank Deborah Heath, Lane Hirabayashi, Jacey Laborte, Larry Lipin, Rick Jobs, Jules Boykoff, Sarah Phillips, Theresa May (editor), and Susanna R. Hill (editorial fellow) for their encouragement and suggestions. Above all, I am very grateful to Chris Wilkes, who read many drafts of this book. He has been most generous with his time, his support, and his editing acumen.

Finally, I would like to acknowledge and thank Pacific University and the National Science Foundation for supporting my fieldwork during the 1990s.

REINVENTING PRACTICE IN A DISENCHANTED WORLD

The truth of our society can be understood as well from the bottom as from the top,[1] but the dominant discourse of our "New Gilded Age,"[2] widely disseminated in late capitalism by those who own the instruments of communication, rests upon an assertion of moral supremacy among the rich. Theorems of these individual achievements, widely believed and endlessly repeated by the rich themselves,[3] are also widely agreed to in the broader community. This self-serving language, extolling the virtues of hard work and sacrifice, provides the ideological framework for the globalization process. It is the language of empire and its moral economy. It is not the language of working people, or of community, of social services, of respect for diversity, or of communal support. Instead the cult of individualism dominates. Not content with controlling most of the world's resources, the rich also appear to want to control the moral high ground.

This book charts the lives of a group of poor urban migrants in Mexico over a period of thirty years as the nation became more closely tied into the structures of global capital, and my informants struggled to survive in Colonia Hermosa. Like the rich, the people I got to know shaped their discussions within a larger narrative focusing on their successful movement from migrant to urban citizen. Their talk is also the language of the heroic individual, so necessary to the ideology and functioning of capital. But, as among the rich, this logic only tenuously connects to the actual material circumstances of their lives.

There is irony at the heart of this story. It is the tale of a people struggling from rural poverty for the chance to be part of the global economy in Oaxaca. For them, the chance to enter the urban proletariat is success indeed, and yet this move places them foursquare on the lowest rung of the global infrastructure, open to exploitation and subjugation. Given the overwhelming conditions in which the poor live, the testaments of *colonia* residents are impressive as well as instructive.

DISENCHANTMENT

In social science, the term "disenchantment" generally is associated with the work of Max Weber, specifically his book *The Protestant Ethic and the Spirit of Capitalism* (1958). Weber set out to investigate the role of religion (in practice) in the emergence of capitalism. He argued that the Protestant ethic fostered an attitude toward the world that contributed to the rise of bourgeois rational capitalism, which for him implied a way of thinking about the world and about social relationships different from that which went before. And what went before was feudalism, slavery, and the primarily noncapitalist forms of rural life (Keyes 2002). In his work on science, Weber argued that the rise of rationalism based on scientific inquiry left no space for spiritual or metaphysical matters.[4] In this way the world became "disenchanted" for people. Rationalism, greed, and science—each working together to form a hermetically sealed ideology—eviscerated other forms of human life and left a sparse residue behind. Weber further argued that the advent of bureaucratic structures might effectively negate the role of the individual.

I use "disenchantment" with a meaning that follows Pierre Bourdieu (1972, 1979a) and his argument that symbolic and cultural capitals, which traditionally have been the key social determinants, have now been superseded by the dominance of economic capital in a world where collective enterprise has given way to individual achievement. This argument has its roots in a discussion of traditional Mexican village life, which continues to be of wide interest, especially in economic anthropology. The argument focuses on the economic and social activities in primarily indigenous Oaxacan villages, where most of my informants originated. While agriculturally based, many people in such villages are also employed in small industries such as weaving, and the making and marketing of mescal and construction materials (Cook 2004: 182–3). As Cook has argued,[5] one crucial problem for scholars is to connect meaning with economic activities: where, in these activities, are the sources of symbolic and cultural capital? As Cook observes, some people nurture "varieties of 'ethnocultural survivalism' that are conceptualized as embedding economic process in a shroud of tradition-enforcing, and identity-forging sociocultural practice." Such communities also have been characterized as those which cooperate and stratify themselves on the basis of the *tequio* (a community work group) and a variety of symbolic and cultural capitals, which are thought to be more important and determinant than cash (Cohen 1998). These theorists are categorized by Cook as "ethnopopulists" (Cook 2004: 182–212). Elsewhere, scholars have argued that underlying any market involvement is commodity production, and that this activity inevitably leads to a community that is stratified and class differentiated. In his study of the peasant economy in Oaxaca with Leigh Binford (1990), Cook argues that villages were long ago transformed into "a commodity economy with complex circuits of value flows and corresponding relations participated in by multiple subjects . . . none of which could be easily identified as 'peasants'" (Cook and Binford 1990: 12–15).

Indeed, a broader reading of the history of indigenous Mexican villages demonstrates that all (so-called) traditional Mexican communities have been stratified; traditional male leaders, or *caciques*, have always carried what might be understood as symbolic capital, such as the burdens of office and the honor of those burdens. In village life, as in city life, honor and prestige are connected to economic and cultural capital, as individual men and their families have traversed the cargo system. In this book I am less concerned about the argument over the nature of peasant communities than I am over the question of *transition*. What I have found is that colonia residents in Oaxaca have decidedly changed their views of community and familial projects, views that were founded in the country, as well as changing by degrees their personal and household practices as they entered city life. Their own words underscore a massive shift in the way they see themselves and the future.

I argue that the community I studied transformed itself from an economy of collective work groups to an economy of individualist action based on a world of money and commodity exchange, rather than a universe that privileged symbolic capital. New practices and changed ideology depend upon entrepreneurial skills. As they lived longer in the colonia, families, not surprisingly, began to shape their broad social practices more closely to the imperatives of the urban capitalist economy. And these changes can be precisely conceptualized as moving from the fully lived—that is, a community in which symbolic and cultural capital competes equally with economic capital—to a world of narrow, economistic thought. This is the world, as Bourdieu puts it, of disenchantment.

MEMORY AND IMAGINATION

The lives of the residents of Colonia Hermosa, clinging to the side of a hill in "suburban" Oaxaca, constitute the center of this story. I structure the book around the narratives they wanted to tell. These are stories of success and perseverance, of family transformation, and of the future that they created for themselves and continue to imagine.

All human stories are embedded in memory, and memories are both individual and collective. Thus, the notion of the "truth" of an account is routinely problematic and is to be found somewhere in the space between an individual's experience and the social field in which memory is formed and understood. Bourdieu's (1972) philosophical work on the dialectic between the "structuring structures" of society and the shape of individual and familial dispositions (qualities he called the "habitus") is instructive here. Anthropologists eager to examine the social practices of individuals and communities look closely at the connection between structures and habitus. Memory and interpretation are colored both by social conditions and by subjective experience. So, making sense of ourselves, our memories, and how we express them is produced through a process that is both social and corporeal.[6] The residents' narratives that are included in this book are thus anchored in a common history that derives from both a shared, lived experience and a collective memory that they constructed with me in an ethnographic setting.

In the 1990s, my informants and I were able to trade and retell stories from all the years since 1968: stories of children, husbands, jobs, anticipations, disappointments, and successes. In this retelling, stories were constructed and reconstructed as a form of social consensus was reached. Then, using this consensus, we were able to chart the changes over these years. This mechanism suggests that not only memory formation is dialectical, but that the very process of ethnographic research itself takes the same form, moving us very decidedly from the objectivism of the past. In the case in point, individual memory can be seen to derive from both the daily events of informants' lives, such as their jobs and other choices they made, as well as from their internal dispositions—their habitus, in the Bourdieuian vocabulary—which serve to orient a person's approach to his or her life. I expand on this general idea in Chapter 2 and focus on the choices and dispositions of one key informant in Chapter 3. But as well as choices and dispositions, residents' memories and their narrative accounts are embedded in their material surroundings and their household settings. The context of social life is thus fully explored in Chapter 4.

POSITIONALITY: THE PERSONAL AND THE ETHNOGRAPHIC

In addition to considering the questions of memory and collective expressions of the past, I hope that in analyzing informants' stories and my narratives that readers will also consider the attributes that researchers and writers carry within them that both structure and give meaning to what they see in the world. By this I refer to the feelings, both personal and ideological, that fashion how we all understand the stories our respondents tell us. The work of the cultural anthropologist is self-consciously personal, and like all scientists, we bring to the field of study our own dispositions, which is why it is crucial that we consider our own positionality when we do our fieldwork.

My own situation with regard to this study is intimately connected to the fact that I have close personal ties to those with whom I have worked. I am sympathetic to the daily struggles and hardships that they endure; I am proud of their successes, but also deeply concerned about the structures of capital that have put them into situations of poverty; and I am worried about their futures as they grow old, as well as the futures of their children and grandchildren as they grow up.

I began my first fieldwork in 1968 as a very young first-year graduate student, when I and other students traveled to study "squatter settlements" in Oaxaca. I gave birth to my son in Oaxaca, and some years later it was my informants who regularly cared for and fed my children when they returned to Oaxaca with their father. Thirty years after my first meeting with Colonia Hermosa residents, we talked about one another's children, we wondered about our grandchildren, and we thought about what might be best for them. We commiserated. We have grown old together. Many years ago we became *compadres* (godparents), and we have been friends and acquaintances over a long period of time. When I again surfaced in Oaxaca from my life in New Zealand, my first marriage well over and my children grown, we were pleased to see one another; there was a pleasant shock of recognition and the equal pleasure of knowing that we were all growing old, parallel in time, together. I was surprised and then gratified that they remembered me, and with such affection.

This warm, personal feeling contrasted sharply with the shock I felt when I saw the city of Oaxaca again in the late 1990s. The space of the city was no longer recognizable to me, primarily because of the new roads and the "great rush of the world"—the pace and scramble of traffic, the hillsides bursting with new colonias, the dust and tumult of new downtown construction sites, the pervasive smell of exhaust fumes, and the sheer noise of it all. The Oaxacan populace filled the sidewalks and streets, working from morning well past the traditional *comida* time of 1 or 2 p.m., and often until 4 p.m., before taking a decent break for their family meal. Family structure, long embedded in social dispositions, had been drastically altered. People were working, it seemed to me, much harder than ever before to piece together the 80 new pesos a day that my compadres told me was the minimum needed to support a family.

The downtown *zócalo* (main square) area, with its traditional Spanish Colonial architecture, had been turned into a "full-on" tourist zone. The business of selling Oaxaca, which had earlier been a partial and incomplete process, had now been fully realized, and the strategic transformation of popular creations into ornaments and marketable items has happened everywhere. Cultural citizenship, as Rosaldo (1994: 402–11) defines it, refers to the "right to be different and to belong in a participatory democratic sense . . . social justice [that] calls for equity among all citizens . . . and the ability to influence one's destiny by having a significant voice in basic decisions." While all manner of indigenous dress and languages are on view in Oaxaca, Rosaldo's requirements of cultural citizenship are simply not being met. Differences in language, dress, and thought are not compatible with the progress of the market except insofar as traditional goods can be bought and sold, thus becoming commodities. In Oaxaca, the process of capitalist modernization and globalized consciousness is twofold and contradictory; it pushes indigenous and traditional Mexican life to the margins, while at the same time bringing the consumable objects from those same lives into the center of the market economy. So far, tourism is Oaxaca's only industry, and while it has brought money into the economy and is responsible for creating many peso millionaires, it also means that Oaxaca is engaged in a process of literally devouring itself.

In the field of cultural anthropology our key research tool is *participant observation*. What this means is that we explore the lived experiences of our informants, and then, after leaving the field, we write about the social conditions of possibility: the effects of, and the limits to, the lived experience. Social science takes as a given the understanding that individuals are shaped, formed, and changed by social conditions. Thus, a certain amount of reflexivity is important and helps to situate any study of everyday life and researchers' interpretations of the lives of their informants.

A PERSONAL INTRODUCTION

I grew up in California, in the Bay Area, in the 1950s and 1960s, a student of language and culture, deeply imbued with the idealism that swirled around the social movements connected to resistance to the Vietnam War, President Johnson's "War on Poverty," and the compelling struggle toward civil rights among African Americans. The most important book that I came across as an undergraduate was Oscar Lewis's *The Children of Sánchez* (1959). After reading it, and in a straightforward fashion, I decided to train as an anthropologist, work with Lewis as much as I could (which I did until his death in 1972), and find a job dealing with the question of urban poverty, which I did in the university setting and also in the Housing Authority offices of Santa Clara County and San Francisco.

Lewis's argument was compelling for the simple reason that my background understanding of poverty, derived from the suburban life of the San Francisco Peninsula in the 1950s and 1960s, did not sit well with me. The familiar argument that explained poverty in that context paralleled that of the captains of the "Gilded Age" as they explained their own wealth. Just as these captains of industry considered themselves full of virtue, the poor were conceived to be morally doubtful. Poverty, it was claimed, arose from the personal failures of those who were poor. Much of this thinking derived from racial and ethnic stereotyping. Thus, poverty was said to result from the lack of a Protestant work ethic, a condition which was endemic to certain communities and therefore immutable to change. This form of racist fatalism allowed white suburban America to discount further thought and action. In the early 1960s, there was little debate about these understandings in white-dominated suburban high schools.

The logic of racism offended me at several levels. First, as a member of a Catholic parish, I could not mesh the teachings of the Church from the New Testament on issues of poverty, especially Christ's teaching on the poor, with the fatalistic and mean-spirited blaming that people used in the everyday world. Second, for all the puffery about American success in the 1950s and the self-congratulatory tone that colored much of the discourse about American society, I could not understand how one category of people, and apparently always the same category of people, managed to act repeatedly against their own self-interest to reproduce poverty and misery in their lives.

Against all the influences around me, I knew that these ideas were wrong, though I had no theoretical armature at hand to construct an alternative understanding. Unlike many academics, I did not come from an intellectual family. Hence, Lewis's book came as a revelation. Lewis explained that living in poverty powerfully structures the way people conceive of a life and strategically shapes the possibilities for that life—how it might unfold. Critics argued that Lewis was blaming the poor for their condition, for being unable to think outside of their world and envision things differently.[7] But I took from Lewis's argument a different, though rather naive message, which was that a structural argument could view people as captured by poverty. Thus, in my view, the structure of poverty was the responsibility of the state, because poverty was structurally embedded in the larger society and was, in fact, necessary to the smooth running of the economy, an economy that was buttressed by the state.[8] I felt that poverty, in general, was not the direct responsibility of individuals, most of whom lived their lives as best they could under difficult circumstances. Thus, I began to see the state as a powerful determining force that sustained and reproduced poverty. I became a determinist—hardly a finished theoretical position, but certainly a way out of the individualist understandings that undergirded the ethnic and class stereotyping of this era.

Then I made my first trip to Colonia Hermosa. What I encountered there, in addition to facing my naiveté and romanticism with regard to the actual lives of the poor, was the sheer genius of the everyday heroic struggles of families in meeting their needs. Being a witness to these lives helped me focus on the question of how it was that they actually survived and sustained themselves each day: what were the choices that they made in the face of overwhelming difficulties of finding work and avoiding poverty? So, while I still felt that the state was accountable for the terrible structural inequities in Mexico, I also understood from the way people shared their stories with me that *they* felt in control of their lives, and that *they* had very particular ideas about how they wanted the future to unfold. They also had strong views about how they might reach some of these goals for at least some of their children, if not for themselves.

I do not mean to imply that they were happy with the Mexican state or its offices; on the contrary, they were cynical and sometimes very angry. But colonia residents did not look to government for help in their lives; how could they? There simply was no help available, except during election years, and for the most obvious and instrumental reasons. Out of their desperation developed collective strength and individual determination. They felt much more powerful than I had understood them to be. This sense of a limited power—that even in the most difficult situations of poverty and overwork, things were possible—drove their energies toward the goal of entering the urban proletariat.

MOVING SOCIAL POSITION

For the Mexican poor, urban life is difficult, but rural life is often impossible. For my informants and their families, it was a necessity for them to migrate to the city, even though they often had no money, no family ties, no jobs, no education, or even, in some cases, fluency in Spanish. Some residents arrived from rural villages speaking only Zapotec, Mazatec, or Mixe. As Bourdieu would put it, they made a virtue out of necessity. In the 1960s, as hard-working, subproletarian squatters, they spoke to me of the *imagined* life that they hoped they and their children would have. This vision of urban life, which was not as yet realized, was one in which their children would be educated, and where they would all have secure jobs and enough money for food, decent housing with potable water and modern plumbing, medical care, and a garden area in which to enjoy their plants, flowers, caged birds, and a few chickens. It was this view, common to all the residents of Colonia Hermosa, that motivated them to work with the community-based tequio,[9] a communal work group that created some of the school buildings, water wells, paths, and streetlights that they came to share.

One might ask where such imagined lives came from, and how they were held in common by people from such different geographical locations across Mexico. Such commonality derives from common experience, from the social construction of everyday life. This commonality is itself produced by myriad structural (political, economic, cultural, and symbolic) forces, which then together, and not without contradictions, create a *doxic,* or taken-for-granted logic. As part of a collective, doxic understanding of what we might term "the legitimate objects of the imagination," we find their common imagined futures coming together to confront an explosive period of urban growth, advanced consumerism, and closer integration into the global market. Colonia residents therefore provided for themselves a historical structure upon which their family stories could be built.

Now, thirty years later, as I write about Colonia Hermosa, both the lives of my informants and my own positionality with regard to their lives has been, in part, reconstructed by a new phase of global capitalism.[10] Within this framework we see the residents no longer as migrants to the city, even though that history is critical, but as permanent citizens of Oaxaca, whose urban logic has shifted from past understandings of community and the uses of symbolic capital through their experiences over thirty years. The story of this transformation provides the focus of the book.

At the time I was writing (summer 2007), conditions in Oaxaca seemed particularly difficult for the poor. In May 2006, teachers were striking for higher wages, and this call led to the occupation of many buildings and streets in Oaxaca's capital city. By October, thousands were routinely taking to the streets, demanding the governor's resignation. Demonstrations, riots, killings, and massive police repression followed. Although some business and civic leaders worked to normalize conditions in 2007, further demonstrations and the use of tear gas were still in evidence on Oaxacan streets in July of that year. The period of sleepy provincial life that had characterized Oaxaca in the past is gone forever.

CONCLUSION

This book is structured in the following way: the first two chapters introduce Colonia Hermosa residents and the places where they live. I also outline the reflexive and participatory nature of the research in order to bring the reader along with me as a joint participant. In Chapter 1, I introduce the colonia and, briefly, Oaxaca. I suggest the reasons why migrants flocked to the city, and bring into focus the dramatic process of building a community on a spare hillside at the edge of town. Chapter 2 reviews the evolution of the research project and its major goals. I discuss the theoretical and practical methodology used, emphasizing Bourdieu's generative structuralism and his key ideas of habitus, field, and practice.

The next four chapters focus on the life stories of colonia residents. In Chapter 3 we meet one of my key informants, "Consuelo," and discuss her life history as an example of the lives of many women in the colonia and the challenges that connect their past with their current situation. The main themes of Chapter 3 are related to the three *calculated strategies* that Consuelo chose to use in order to construct what she considers to be a successful life: the strategies of prayer, work, and marriage. Such strategies are routinely drawn upon in the lives of the women of the community.

Chapter 4 reviews the process that a series of colonia families used to build and develop their homes and family compounds. I emphasize the critical connection between identity and landscape that exists for the residents of Hermosa. In most cases, the changes in homes and their contents stand for them as clear, material testament to their increased economic success over the years. Chapter 5 examines the structuring nature of work on the lives of informants. Work is the seminal activity that connects the self and personal dispositions to the larger social arena. Work narratives illustrate how the structure of colonia stratification is revealed through the way that symbolic, social, and economic capital is used and valued, and how it has changed over time. The types of labor that *colonos* engaged in served to establish an early social hierarchy that rapidly dissolved over the years into new forms of hierarchical structures.

In Chapter 6 I relate stories from a series of women and their families, focusing on how they helped one another to meet daily food and child-care needs in the early decades of the colonia. Overall, we see how strategies for using symbolic and social capital were transformed into the need for obtaining economic capital. Also reviewed are emerging forms of family strategies, strategies that have survived into the present and which are quite different from those used by the original networks of neighbors, friends, and compadres.

Finally, Chapter 7 draws together what I take to be the most powerful conclusions from the study. The compelling belief of Colonia Hermosa residents is that they have succeeded. They experience success routinely by overcoming their day-to-day travails. They gain success in an often-unforgiving economic structure, and achieve success also in keeping their families intact, despite the fact that many migrate back and forth to the United States. What the deeper logic of these narratives helps us to do is to bring us in touch with a profound human need, with how our lives and their lives are connected through global capitalism, and with how they (in their own terms) have attained a level of success from impossible circumstances.

Given that Mexico is our neighbor, and that we are connected to millions of its inhabitants through the continuous process of migration across our mutual border, there is no more important problem to understand. I believe that these stories can help us to think anew about what to value in the world, and what we might do to help solve the enduring problems of global poverty and injustice. Toward that end, I have included chapter summaries and discussion questions that are designed to be helpful in the classroom.

CHAPTER I

COLONIA LIFE IN OAXACA

A BIRTH IN THE FAMILY

AT 9:45 ON A NOVEMBER MORNING in 1969, Gloria gave birth to her sixth child, a severely deformed little boy who was born with a perfect body, but whose head lacked a crown (partial anencephaly). Gloria herself suffered from the birth and needed blood transfusions. By early afternoon the child had been taken home from the clinic in a box by his aunt via one of the local second-class buses. A box was used because of what neighbors might say about such an ugly child. The family was both embarrassed and horrified. Meanwhile, Gloria lay in her room in the clinic. Her bloodstained clothing was still in the corner of her room; her blood transfusion bag was hung on a coat rack. No one wanted to tell her about the little boy for fear that, as a consequence, she might suffer from an illness called *susto*.[1]

Later that afternoon, a group of Gloria's family went to visit her. Although they still did not tell her about the child, they discussed it among themselves outside her room. The child was still alive and was being given chamomile tea. Some of the family members argued to let him die. Others argued that their responsibility was to life, and to do anything intentionally to hurt the child would be counted by God as a mortal sin. At that moment, the doctor came to visit his clinic, and he discussed the child with the family. He said that for 500 pesos (about $50.00 US at the time), he felt sure that he could "fix" the boy. Again, the family argued about the kind of life the child would have since he was deformed and had been born into a poor family. Others argued that not to do everything possible would be a sin in the eyes of God. The problem, however, solved itself since the child died shortly after the conversation.

After a look at Gloria, who still needed blood transfusions, the doctor again demanded 500 pesos, this time for her to remain in the clinic. Not to stay in the clinic would have severely endangered her health. The family borrowed the money that night from compadres and paid the bill. When Gloria was ready to come home, her sisters and her other children cleaned the house and burned *copal* (incense) to make sure that there was nothing left of the *cangrena* (the infected atmosphere that could poison her blood)[2] left by the child's corpse. If there had been something left, Gloria in her weakened state would be vulnerable and could become very ill.

After a time, reflecting on this crisis, the family agreed that the doctor was excellent because he had cured Gloria. They did not expect anything more in terms of his behavior toward the child, nor in terms of kindness towards the patient and her family. The family believed that the infant's birth defect was due to the hepatitis Gloria suffered during her pregnancy, which she says was contracted from a dirty needle at the Centro de Salud during a vaccination. The fact that the doctor at the private clinic demanded so much money in such a short time did not shock them. The doctor's actions were not recognized as cruel, nor as poor medical practice, but rather as a set of entirely legitimate actions. The family felt proud to have been in his clinic, and proud that such a doctor would help them. For them it was a kind of social capital to be in a private clinic instead of in the government-run Hospital Civil or the Social Security Hospital.

SURVIVING IN THE CITY

This chapter introduces the reader to the squatter settlement of Colonia Hermosa in the city of Oaxaca, and it is appropriate that we start with this story. This account exemplifies the challenges faced by the poor in Oaxaca, Mexico, when they seek medical care. Similar stories are repeated many times. Economic circumstances, as well as limited knowledge and few social resources, shape the entire medical experience for the poor. This doctor, like so many others in Oaxaca, manages two clinics in town: one for the middle-class and one for the poor. The fees in each clinic are the same, but the care and services differ enormously. The birth of this child took place in the clinic for the poor. The doctor is proud of his clinic and the help that he "gives" to the poor. He sees no contradiction between the cost of his services and the fact that his poor clients pay as much as his wealthier clients, but do not receive the same quality of care.

In addition to the challenge of giving birth and providing for a new child, families are faced with the cost of medical bills, which is a part of the symbolic violence that the poor endure from many in the medical establishment. The rest is connected to the insensitive treatment they receive and the disdain with which many doctors treat their poorer patients. Lack of adequate, affordable medical care reveals part of the broad structure of domination within which the poor exist. This particular family, faced with a child near death and little medical guidance or money, called upon what they had: spiritual guidance from Catholic and traditional resources, and medical remedies from traditional medicine. What is revealed in their conversations are the ideological structures that support their thinking: Catholicism, spirituality, traditional herb-based medicine, and economic and social constraints all shape their beliefs. A close reading of this story reveals how the family failed to recognize the symbolic violence that they endured from the doctor and the clinic. Even though they misinterpreted this important part of their interaction with the doctor, it is nevertheless a significant narrative thread woven throughout their experiences. They are, as Gramsci reminds us in his discussion of hegemony,[3] party to their own domination, accepting of it and compliant with its consequences. The failure to recognize symbolic violence, as the narrative above outlines, is peppered throughout the lives of colonia residents even today, and serves to establish and reproduce the structures of domination between social classes.

When I first began work in Colonia Hermosa, I wanted to learn how it was that people were able to survive economically in the city. One issue that consistently arose in their conversations was that of the future: how they imagined it would be, and the strategies they were going to use to get there. In the mid-1990s, after a long hiatus while I lived in New Zealand, I returned to the colonia to find out how their lives had evolved with regard to social place and self-identity. Social scientists would define the original class positions of colonia residents as subproletarian, which, in a general way, refers to those people who work outside the normal structures of paid employment, and who make their living on the edges of the economy. For instance, some colonia residents sold their labor to construction contractors each day from a street corner, while others sold food from the sidewalks along downtown streets. There are many jobs like these in developing countries. They are casual, outside any formal labor contracts or structures of civil life. And while the transformations people experienced are complex, the fundamental economic shift that people in this world hope for is to move from this subproletarian status to membership in the urban working class. Not only did their income and jobs change in this move, but also their *sense* of themselves was transformed. Informal work became formal work. Colonia residents came to live in a larger world in which an elaborate structure of social and economic capital enshrouded them, much of it beyond their previous experience. In order to account for this particular change, we must investigate the central theoretical and empirical question: What is the connection between ideology and self-identification and the larger society, and the material conditions in which people live? How does this allow them to survive?

THE HISTORICAL CONTEXT OF OAXACA

One of the principal features of the Spanish conquest of America is its urban character. In Mesoamerica, and specifically in Oaxaca, urban centers are not new.[4] The city of Oaxaca lies in the largest plain in the center of the state, which is created by three overlapping valleys. The Atoyac River separates the city's eastern and western sides. On the surrounding hills to the west, just outside of the modern city of Oaxaca, lie the ruins of Monte Albán, one of the most ancient urban centers in the New World.

In the sixteenth and seventeenth centuries, the elite class of this community was comprised of merchants, high government officials, senior clergy, and landowners. The middle class was formed from the ranks of physicians, lawyers, minor officials, and the lesser clergy. The "upper" lower group consisted of high-status groups such as pharmacists, musicians, and traders. The lower class consisted largely of peons, servants, and poorly skilled workers such as carpenters, fireworksmakers, small traders, and weavers (Chance 1978; Wolf 1959).

Oaxaca became a favorable environment for the successful accumulation of capital because the indigenous population provided a cheap source of labor, and because merchants were eager to establish new markets. It is very clear that even during the early years of city development, peasants exchanged their labor for wages, and their wages for commodities. Chance (1978) concludes that many features of early Oaxaca gave the appearance of a developing (merchant) capitalist economy, particularly with the emergence of an unstable urban elite. This class gained its status through newly evolving forms of social mobility

FIGURE 1.1. Oaxacan street scene, 1970

in which the "rules of the game" were as yet unclear (Chance 1978: 200). This structural framework, dependent on the complex relationship between various elements in the city, and the penetration of the city by the rural and suburban sectors, is at the core of the contemporary social structure, with its parallel forms of development.

After the Mexican Revolution of 1910–20, Oaxaca remained a provincial city with no single dominant industry, but with a large and complex population of communities differentiated by their languages and ethnic identities. By the late 1940s, Oaxaca had become connected to other major Mexican centers through the completion of the Pan-American Highway. By the 1990s the highway had been reengineered and enlarged, allowing for quicker travel to Mexico City by car or bus. Since that time there have been two major changes in the city of Oaxaca. First, the population has increased substantially, and second, the city's economic base has changed, with tourism now the major commercial interest. As both the population and tourism have increased, the service sector has also expanded dramatically, absorbing many residents of Colonia Hermosa.

Beyond tourism, Oaxaca functions largely the same today as in colonial and postcolonial times: the city continues to be the major state center for government and business, and the dominant market center for outlying indigenous villages. Physically, Oaxaca retains some of its colonial appearance—especially within the tourist zone in the center of the city—but increasingly its daily rhythms are being reshaped to meet the needs of an emerging business economy.

While traditional dress, languages, and crafts continue to be a living part of society, more and more of these indigenous remnants are being transformed into items of popular culture that are, on the whole, created to be consumed as tourist commodities. Today, as before, Oaxaca's population is stratified on the basis of material and symbolic power based on occupation, marriage networks, language, and race.

MIGRATION PATTERNS TO OAXACA

Migrants, both in the past and the present, enter the city's economy to work as artisans, vendors, and service personnel. Migrants and "suburbs" are not new in Oaxaca, but what has changed under modernization is the nature of the city's dominant economic logic. Thus, while the alienation of land rights began during the period of the Spanish conquest, the transition from the fully lived to the economic mode of kinship and religion is seen only in the latest phase of modern capital, and is a response to the demands of a specific social formation. The precise pressures that new inhabitants experience when they settle in the city exacerbate this problem.

The structure of contemporary Mexican society is such that many families cope with difficult rural economic situations by migrating to urban areas in search of jobs and economic security. Because migrants often lack skills and expertise, and yet most industries increasingly rely on advanced technology, the rate of unemployment and underemployment is exceedingly high for these groups. Many new migrants settle in squatter settlements outside of the city or live in inner-city slums. Most have little choice. Almost all of them, in some way or another, are forced to live in overcrowded conditions with few basic amenities.

Jobs selling articles on the street are a common way to begin. People sell all kinds of things, from bags of chewing gum to food, pencils, and lottery tickets. Those who do find steady employment become part of the urban working class of Mexico. However, even with steady jobs, they often face inadequate city services in the settlements.

Despite great problems, poor housing, and severely marginal work, the comparative concentration of wealth in cities remains a magnet for unskilled workers from rural areas. In a typical account of urban poor studies in Mexico in the 1970s, Larissa Adler Lomnitz (1977: 35–61) examined the effects of the wealth of urban areas on rural dwellers. She lists five key factors that were critical to residents' decisions to move to urban areas today (2007)—factors that were also important in the lives of my own informants. These same factors have also led migrants to roam even farther afield, to work in the United States.

1. The relative working conditions are improved for industry and workers in the city.
2. Public health services are more modern and more readily available than they are in the countryside.
3. Roads, telephone lines, and television reception are much improved in urban areas.
4. The educational system offers a much better quality education in the cities.
5. Communication between cities and rural areas is easier and more reliable now than ever before.[5]

The attractions of cities, along with the harsh realities of rural living—such as population growth, fragmentation of rural holdings, and soil erosion—combine to foster large migrations. By the year 2000, the shantytown or squatter settlement population of Latin American cities had grown to between 100 and 150 million people. Marginal urban populations increase at a rate of 15 percent per annum. Given the size of many of these cities, this growth is staggering. Sao Paolo is estimated to have 18 million inhabitants; Mexico City in 2005 had 19.1 million. The growth of this new urban population has far exceeded the cities' capabilities to cope. Three problems are dominant in this regard: underemployment and unemployment; poor health maintenance and nutrition; and substandard education and housing. These three conditions characterize the lives of the poor in Latin American cities, and are so widespread that they defy logical solutions.

Such conditions also exist extensively in Mexico, and Oaxaca and Colonia Hermosa are no exception. Nowadays, such problems provide further impetus to migrate a second time, from Oaxaca to the United States, in search of better work and more promising futures. Thus, while *their* parents migrated to the city of Oaxaca in the rural-urban pattern, many of the children of the most recent generation, and especially the young men, will make the journey to the North.

If we want to know how the Oaxacan communities under study first came into being, the answer lies far away from the city, in the rural villages and district capitals (Rees et al. 1991). Most migrants came from mestizo villages in the valley and from Zapotec villages; some came from Mazatec, Mixtec, Mixe, and Trique villages, and others from Oaxacan coastal villages. Small numbers of migrants started out from the surrounding areas of Puebla, and a very few from Mexico City. Most of the colonias, which are located on the outskirts of the city, began as residential areas for the poor and were first referred to as *colonias pobres* or *colonias populares*. They were established as squatter settlements but eventually organized their resources in some fashion, at which time incorporation into the city normally took place. They are now characterized as suburbs and have been formally incorporated into the city. As a result they have bus service, schools, market centers, and access to city water and electricity. Most of the houses have been rebuilt from very humble beginnings into brick and concrete structures, and many have walls built around their courtyards.

According to an early survey by Arthur Murphy and Alex Stepick (1991: 47), 70 percent of the migrants to Oaxaca have moved from their birthplace directly to the city, with Zapotec populations forming the largest distinctively separate ethnic group. Fewer than 10 percent of migrants came from outside of the state. Of those, two-thirds came from other urban centers. Colonia Hermosa reflects these trends: the population is based on an older generation of migrants who came to settle there during the late 1950s, 1960s, and early 1970s. Their children are city born. When the initial generation of settlers founded Colonia Hermosa, most residents were in their early twenties and generally living in free union marriages. This pattern confirms the later work of Murphy and Stepick, which gave the overall proportion of such households in the urban settlements as 83 percent (1991: 48).

Given its initial status as a squatter settlement and its geographical location, Colonia Hermosa could be likened to a buffer zone between the subproletarian world of migrants and the proletarian world of the modern city. In this zone, residents attempt to construct a social space within which they work to establish basic support systems to contend with daily necessities. The strategic importance of neighborly help networks and self-help political groups is critical to the initial development of such a settlement. One must remember that the colonia was first populated by families from many Oaxacan regions (not just one) and by residents from northern states such as Puebla and Mexico City, as well as from the inner city of Oaxaca. What initially gave the com-

FIGURE 1.2. Colonia Hermosa, 1970

FIGURE 1.3. Colonia Hermosa, 1999

munity its coherence were the needs that each household group had of each other.[6] The important point here is that while colonia families had none of the shared experiences that normally exist in village life (none of the taken-for-granted or doxic knowledge of a particular village), they did share a sense of self-identity through their basic needs as migrants. It was upon these shared needs that they were able to band together and build Colonia Hermosa. Sometimes language was a problem, as often an indigenous language was the first language of older family members and had the effect of further isolating them from mainstream Mexico. This challenge was ameliorated through the linguistic help of their younger family members, and their own practical need to bond together with their neighbors to "get on" with life in the city.

By 1968, when I first arrived, Colonia Hermosa was a large squatter settlement with a rather complex community structure. Its population in 1968 numbered about three hundred families. As one entered the city along the Pan-American Highway from the north, the colonia was one of the first visible shantytowns. There were two dirt roads and several footpaths that ranged high up onto the hillside. Upon entering the colonia, I noticed the effects of community work: five communal water taps in the middle of the road, a school being constructed, and a scattering of electric street lamps. Bordering this scene, in a way that seemed to announce the colonia's existence to all passersby, were two rows of plastered and brightly painted houses facing the street, a row of house fronts that continued on up the road until it became a path on the rise of the hillside. Some of the houses had small shops in their living rooms, with their windows serving as shop counters. In the 1960s, as now, the colonia's geographical boundaries touched other colonias populares composed of similar house types and whose residents worked in similar low-paying jobs as rural school teachers, carpenters, store clerks, tortilla vendors, ice cream vendors, second-class bus and truck drivers, day laborers in construction, women who took in laundry, and women who sold food door-to-door.

In 1969, the residents described Colonia Hermosa as being divided into four areas, each with its own character. The first section, which had the school, water taps, and most of the shops, had an upper and lower division. The lower division, where the landscape was flatter and offered easy access to the highway, was where the earliest and most prosperous residents lived. The second section was divided from the first by a ravine. It lay closer to the city and was also divided into an upper and lower section. Geography and class mapped simply on to one another: the higher up the hill, the more difficult the social conditions. Newcomers had to go higher. Generally, residents in the second sections were poorer than those of the first section. This is still true today. Nowadays any new house sites must be built out of the side of a very high and steep part of the hill. The new arrivals, say earlier residents, are largely indigenous Trique,[7] from the Oaxacan region of the Mixteca Alta, who work in the city selling their weaving to tourists.

Colonia Hermosa is situated directly against the Pan-American Highway, allowing residents easy access to city buses. There were two colonia streets in 1968. They were wide, unpaved, and turned into many diverging footpaths as they continued up the hill. One of the basic difficulties with colonia streets is the flooding that occurs during the wet season, when rain drenches the city on a daily basis. In the colonia, the water runs down the hill in heavy rivulets in the streets and paths. Before residents had a proper sewage system, the runoff would clean the hillsides of animal and human waste. Now paved streets and pathways penetrate the entire colonia and continue into the surrounding neighborhoods, but the rain gutters and drains are far too shallow to cope with the deluge. Water still runs down the hillside because of inadequate attention to drainage and road construction.

Colonia houses were first made of wattle and daub, with the occasional concrete room. Now housing types vary from substantial brick, cement-covered adobe houses with patios plus three or four rooms, to less substantial brick and adobe houses with fewer rooms, and, finally, a few shacks (*jacales*) made of wattle and daub, with tarpaper roofs. These houses, often used by new residents, echo the older constructions of the 1960s and 1970s, when residences were first established.

BUILDING A COMMUNITY

An apt description of the early days in the settling of Colonia Hermosa and other colonias along the highway in Oaxaca is provided by Pierre Bourdieu:

> On the edges of the cities of Africa and South America there are economic universes which act as a sort of buffer between the sub proletariat and the modern world. Their fundamental law seems to be the same as governs individual practices: the absence of predictability and calculability. The poorest and the most bewildered find there a number

of safeguards which enable them to achieve a precarious equilibrium, at the lowest level, in the absence of any calculation—mutual help among kinsmen and neighbors which burnishes assistance in money or kind during the search for work, or unemployment, sometimes the job itself; a shared living space and kitchen which guarantee subsistence to the most destitute, with the pooling of wages and joint expenditure tending to compensate for the irregularity and smallness of each income; credit based on trust, etc. (Bourdieu 1979: 68–69).

Before Colonia Hermosa was incorporated into city structures during the period 1968–1974, families helped one another through collective action and networks to accomplish many of the goals that each had for securing a better standard of living. Households created alliances with one another through the Mesa Directiva (the community decision-making board, which directed projects) and the tequio, or community work group. Residents also created personal alliances through the system of *compadrazgo* (godparenthood). Relationships were cemented through use of a variety of political, symbolic, and cultural capitals. This created a sense of shared identity for residents, which helped to make Colonia Hermosa into a community. The self-help activities that characterized the early periods of colonia development can be interpreted as a transformed style resulting from the alliance of traditional patterns of rural life (such as the tequio) and the necessary contemporary response to the demands of the city. However, the origin of the colonia is not as seamless as this account might imply. In fact, the community grew out of an intense argument between two factions that ended in a court battle, and jail for one of the main participants.

The initial period of Colonia Hermosa settlement (1959–1967) was fraught with emotionally charged confrontations between two residential groups, resulting in disagreements and rivalries lasting thirteen years. The arguments arose from problems of land ownership and occurred between those who did not have land titles and those who did. One group had bought land from a local teacher who had become a developer, and these people held "title" to their home plots. There were considerably fewer of these titleholders than there were squatters. The story told by the residents—of either side—had the same narrative core: a Oaxacan schoolteacher (whom I will call Méndez) formed Colonia Hermosa in the late 1950s and early 1960s. He decided upon the name and the general territory that the settlement would occupy, though it later expanded its boundaries. Because Méndez had wanted to become a property developer, he negotiated the rights to part of the El Fortín hillside, which lay just outside of the city. He argued later that he had purchased the land that now forms the lower and middle first section of the colonia from a lawyer who had, in turn, claimed to be the sole owner.

Having achieved this control, Méndez then attempted to sell sections of land through radio advertisements aimed at the urban poor of Oaxaca and rural villagers seeking to migrate to the city. As each plot was purchased, the new owner was given a "title." Approximately thirty such titles were sold. Other individuals and families who had heard the radio ads also took up residence on the hillside as squatters without title, some of them on land allegedly owned by Méndez. This ambiguity in ownership created problems between residents. Titled owners resented the squatters and claimed that they had no rights in Colonia Hermosa. Squatters argued that the land was theirs because they had occupied the land peacefully over a number of years.[8] This second group of residents hoped that out of the mix of conflicting questions about land ownership and legal wrangling, the government would federalize the land as irregular urban land (*tierra de nadie*) and give residents political recognition. According to DeWalt et al. (1994), the majority of land upon which colonia populares were constructed in Oaxaca *was* irregular urban land. Because several people who had no clear title claimed the land, the land was federalized, and then residents were allotted titles by the government. This process took several years, during which Sr. Méndez was found guilty of land fraud and was jailed, while at the same time the family of Enrique Guzmán, the chief political broker who brought Sr. Méndez to the notice of the law, became both successful and wealthy.

At this historical juncture, a voluntary work group met their neighborhood goals of securing communal water, three or four streetlights, and their first schoolroom. For many colonia projects, including the installation of streetlights, the government provided the materials, and residents provided the labor. When working on a very large project, such as a community water tank (not potable water), day laborers were hired to supplement tequio-based workers. Residents could also contribute money (2–5 pesos each) to hire day laborers instead of contributing their own labor.

The local office of the ruling political party, the Partido Revolucionario Institutional (PRI), and the PRI elected officials, such as the governor and local representatives, helped to secure building materials, including streetlights, water pipes, materials for the school, and finally the school itself. Their help was especially forthcoming during an election year. Oaxacan state governors Bravo Ahuja (1968–1970) and Gómez Sandoval (1970–1976), and the president of Mexico, Luís Echeverría (1970–1976), were tolerant of squatters in Oaxaca so long as the land selected was federal land and the migrants appeared to be "reasonably well organized" (Murphy and Stepick 1991: 113). Colonia Hermosa benefited from this policy.

The exchanges between government officials and Colonia Hermosa residents carry with them interesting interpretations. First, they may be read in a straightforward fashion as the transfer of goods in exchange for labor and political support. However, this type of exchange also tells us something about the *social relations of capital* when considering the various celebrations of completed projects; first, such gifts from the government to the colonia always occurred around elections for local, state, and federal offices. As election time approached, the tempo of political activity heightened, and candidates, along with their representatives, began to identify themselves more and more with residential associations and community services. Promises were made for street repairs, potable water, and sewage systems. Celebrations of completed projects were always structured around the schedules and needs of officials. Colonia Hermosa's Mesa Directiva would always sponsor a fiesta, and local women would cook and set up the dining area. This usually took place in a small warehouse owned by the head of the Mesa Directiva (Sr. Guzmán). When government officials arrived, everyone lined up in a row but held back, men with their eyes and heads lowered, holding their hats in front of them. Women, except for those few who were part of the Mesa, were always in the back cooking area. Most often the officials who were being honored did not stay for the meal, but instead, after shaking hands and enjoying one drink, they were whisked off back to the city; as a matter of fact, I cannot remember a time when they did remain to enjoy the meal. What was played out in front of me was the clear, traditional pattern of *patron-client* relationships. Thus, for me, the exchange reflected deep roots into the past *patrón-peón* relationships reminiscent of hacienda and rural village social structures.

During the early stages of development, the Mesa Directiva was instrumental in organizing colonia residents, and community development was substantial. The establishment of basic services also meant that residents themselves could feel confident of their community and its place within the city. Colonos (residents) often voiced the opinion that their community had progressed further than neighboring settlements. They often said that they might be *gente humilde* (humble people), but they had built what they had on their own. They believed that their initiative and hard work had finally paid off. It was at this historical juncture that colonia politics became a framework around which the city later recognized Colonia Hermosa as part of the city, a suburb.

As late as 1981 many sections of land had not been regularized. In August and September, colonia residents accused the president of the Mesa Directiva (no longer Guzmán) of corruption and complained to the local newspaper, *Noticias*, that she had misspent the funds that had been collected to help residents gain title to their land. Finally, in the late 1980s, land titles for existing residents were regularized through the city government. It is not clear if the new residents who are now cutting house sites out of the upper reaches of Colonia Hermosa will be given titles in the near future.[9]

CONCLUSION

It should be very clear that Colonia Hermosa itself was founded as part of the broader search for life in the city, and that the process of finding housing and securing land titles was one of the community's defining problems. Even in a well-established colonia such as Hermosa, there were no guarantees to land titles or city services. In securing these benefits for the majority of Hermosa residents, the members of the colonia and the Mesa Directiva won a major battle, which was to advantage residents and their children for years into the future. And, as will be made clear in later chapters, owning title to their land allowed residents to sell and purchase other houses and vacant lots in the city, or to remain living in their initial house on their own land, thereby never having to worry about rent payments or mortgages. Thus gaining title provided residents with, in most cases, a large plot of land on which their children built their own homes. The original inhabitants rarely had to raise the capital to purchase land.

More fundamentally, the establishment of title, the ownership of land, and the gaining of a permanent domicile created the necessary baseline for a viable urban existence. It provided the material circumstances for their launch into the urban working class, and it offered a new foundation for the emergence of an urban sensibility that was to shape community life for many years to come.

CHAPTER 2

CREATING THE OBJECT OF STUDY

THE SUBJECT OF SUCCESS

IN THE 1960S ISABEL and her family were new to the city of Oaxaca; both she and her husband were from indigenous villages in the high-lands—one Zapotec, one Mazatec. They met and married in the city of Oaxaca and moved to Colonia Hermosa. By the early 1970s Isabel was working at home making food to sell and sewing dresses for the market. Her husband, with the help of their eldest son, sold popsicles from a cart on the street. In the late 1970s and early 1980s, while many residents of Colonia Hermosa were "moving up" the economic ladder, Isabel and her family remained in the same difficult economic posi-tion. To account for their inability to take part in certain businesses and social ventures, Isabel would say, "People like us don't do these sorts of things." However, by 1990, through a happy convergence of economic changes in Oaxaca, help from grown and working children, and the fact that their employer offered to sell them his equipment, Isabel's husband and older son started their own business of producing, as well as selling, popsicles. Their equipment consists of two freezers and the tubs to mix the popsicles. They also have the popsicle carts that others now push through the city and the marketplace selling their wares. By 2000, Isabel had taken over the business from her husband, and she now works with her son. They have rented a storefront space close to the central market, and it is there that they produce popsicles and store their equipment. This family now considers themselves to be fully entitled citizens, no longer migrants, and certainly not *indios*. While their village ties and language are still important to the family's older generation, this aspect of their identity is clearly second to their material successes.

This chapter focuses on the nature of the research process itself, and the theoretical and methodological strategies I have followed. I concentrate on the "object of study" and the theoretical apparatus, following that used by Bourdieu. I also pay close attention to the methods I employ to construct ethnographic accounts.

I investigate changes in the lives of colonia settlers as they face daily challenges of survival. I ask: Can we say that this group of residents from the squatter settlement has moved from the position of subproletarians into the working class? If so, how is it that they came to feel "entitled," and how have they have honed their strategies of urban life to the point that they have moved their lives in an upward trajectory? Finally, how is it that we are to understand their stories? Are they simply stories of individual success by people who "pull themselves up by their bootstraps"? Are they stories whose protagonists fail to recognize class structures and personal agency? Or, as I argue, are they narratives that reveal a complex process of social construction, and a recombination of identities with regard to their relationships to a variety of social fields and capitals? This is the book's central argument.

The account that begins this chapter illuminates two parallel processes at work: a change in material circumstances and a change in self-identification, which allows inhabitants to both perceive things anew and to take up the opportunities that come their way. On one hand, this is a success story that happened over thirty years, if one compares the present-day material situation to that of the family's resources in 1968. Much of this change is due to the fact that a new generation is now working (in addition to their parents), and most of them contribute to familial income. But, on the other hand, can we not wonder also if they have now been fully colonized by the logic of the economy, and, from that position, have restructured their notions of individual and community, feel now entitled, but thereby fail to recognize structures of domination?

THE OBJECT OF STUDY: THINKING ABOUT SUCCESS

I begin this methodological inquiry by introducing the key people involved: the women and men whose life stories I have collected. I have focused on their ideas of success, the central story in their narrative. Their ideas are critical to this journey we are examining and enable us to understand their journey toward self-identity and class transformation *as they define it*. Their views about success play an integral part in structuring the research endeavor. The quotations make clear that each person has his or her own idea of success, and how it is to be measured in their lives and in the lives of their children. What are also strikingly clear are the commonalities in the discourse of success: a practical education, hard work, family, and the use of religious thinking are all central themes. Such common dispositions need to be accounted for with regard to the social logic that dominates family and personal attitudes, as well as those that derive from the broader social economy of Oaxaca. As Canclini (1993) notes, capitalist modernization both appropriates and destroys: if one is to survive and thrive in the world of advanced capitalism and globalized culture, there are strategies that one must cultivate, and a community wisdom that one must accept and invite into one's heart.

After hearing from many residents that they had been very successful over the past twenty or so years, I asked a question about their idea of success, and how one was to become successful. Here is a selection of responses:

What I want is for my grandchildren to study. Those who don't will have to study a short career like *belleza* (beauty school) or *costura* (dressmaking), or learn to drive a truck, and get a license, and all the proper papers so that they can work. (Aída, age 70)

For me the fundamental success of a family is the spirit and the unity of the family. If a family lives together, it is successful, because where one is affectionate or finds affection, everyone is united. But also success comes from your hands, as they say in the land of my grandparents, no? One must work hard. If you want something, you will get it. Desire is power. I think that Mexicans don't have a vision of the future that Americans have. What the Mexicans have is the *corazón* [heart]; this is what we choose with, not reason. If we want to continue going ahead, we need to work hard and to better ourselves materially. You have to dedicate yourself to work and to family. (Margarita, age 60)

Mexico has to educate and to teach, and to give people the skills they need to create and to produce. All young people should go to school, to the technical college or to college prep. This will teach them some kind of work. Then, if they want to, they can continue on. But with school, they will have another vision of the world. Right now I don't believe in the government, so for this reason we Mexicans only believe in our own work. (Manuel, age 45)

The dreams I have for my children are that they will study and that they will be good Christians. To help oneself to succeed, one must be humble, to want to work and to dedicate oneself to work. I feel good right now, but I want my children to go further. You have to think. No one wants to stay poor but you have to plan. You have to study or work to learn. You have to want to get ahead. There are many opportunities and work available. But you have to want to work hard. (Rosa, age 43)

These responses seem to be cut from the same mold. From 1968 to 1974 my informants continually said that the important issues were the necessity of schooling and job preparation, living a good Christian life through hard work, family responsibility, and the love of God. Today, these same individuals focus just as often on these same achievements: the work of the individual, the importance of education, being a good Christian, and the centrality of the family. The main difference over the years in their conceptualization of the pathway to success can be found in their increased emphasis on individual achievement, and the ability to make strategic choices regarding jobs and income. Family still matters, both materially and ideologically, but individual achievement has come to dominate, at least on the surface. For those who have missed their chances, the cause, according to my informants, is by and large the failure of the individual, not the larger economic or social structures. The opportunities, they say, are there; one must only *aprovecharlos*, or take advantage of them. This, I think, is their testament to the power of the state and of the market, which argues in favor of the individual, and which drew the urban poor, and these families in particular, to Oaxaca some thirty years ago. Structures of domination and the market call out of the individual certain actions beyond family and community life. Thus, what their stories demonstrate methodologically is that identities and social practices are constructed through the dialectic between personal dispositions and the external reality of objective structures, between individuals and the world that surrounds them. Such structures inhabit all of our lives, as the inhabitants' comments about success demonstrate.

The array of hopes for the future that Colonia Hermosa residents have, and their relationships with outside institutions and one another, are captured within everyday practices and events that emerge from their accounts. These aspirations constitute the major object of this study. What one can hear in their words, here and throughout the text, are two voices. The first is a lyrical voice used when they are talking about family loyalty and when they mention spiritual matters. The other is a practical voice that they use to discuss everyday work, reflecting a struggle for daily survival, for seeking strategies to obtain good jobs, to keep their children in school, to care for their grandchildren, to provide for health care, and to pay bills. As part of this second voice, you will hear over and over again the taken-for-granted notion that it is up to the individual to work hard and to take advantage of what is possible, so that they might succeed in life. It is this taken-for-granted and renewed idea of the individual that has grown over the past thirty years, and it is now the key element in their ideology of success. However, interesting as this is, it is not the key to their actual material success. That aspect of success still depends to a great extent on the power of the extended family and, in some respects, on the community of neighbors and local networks. Often informants do not discuss their dependency on their families. In fact, they seem to not recognize the family help that is, or has been, needed for them to accomplish things individually. This is an interesting sociological point that is discussed further in Chapter 6.

THEORY AND METHODS

As everyone is aware, over the past decade issues surrounding underdevelopment, globalization, and women's rights have surfaced in the general media, particularly with regard to the North American Free Trade Agreement (NAFTA) and the World Trade Organization. Such issues as human rights and economic progress, not to mention those related to environmental sustainability, have rightly become part of our generalized discourse. Historically, the fields of cultural and social anthropology have concerned themselves with these issues in such a way that focuses on individual households and community groups, and their relationship to the decisions and practices of international business and government. The central methodological question raised here is, of course, how to tie personal action and choices to social structures to be able to account for social practice. It comes as no surprise to most people that we all live within an environment structured, in part, by the hegemony of first world economies; we see the evidence of this every day, in our own lives, through what we consume, where and how we manage the workplace, and how we take care of our health, our families, and our bank balances. Such everyday practices must respond to larger societal structures, but they also reflect our personal, family, and class *habitus*,[1] which, if you like, shapes the life possibilities and the choices that we make. Our present historical situation is one in which there is a permanent, and some would say necessary, discrepancy between economic dispositions as they are reflected in the media (thus instigating the desire of consumers) and the economic or material world in which we all live. This discrepancy is all the more the case in areas where third world and First Nation[2] peoples live.

The theoretical apparatus that I employ identifies *social fields* in which, given institutional power and personal histories, my informants have struggled to find their place and imagined their futures. I apply Pierre Bourdieu's (1972, 1990b) theoretical and methodological use of the concepts of *field, habitus,* and *capital.* The most exciting aspect of Bourdieu's work is that it allows the researcher to deal with the problem of connecting ideology and personal practice to larger societal structures. That is, it provides a practice-theoretical methodology which mediates subjectivities and economic structures, and which attends closely to the lived practices of the inhabitants in question. This means that as we look at informants' everyday practices we can theoretically connect a persons' habitus to the fields in which they struggle for the various capitals that make a fundamental difference to their lives.

In this study, we are mapping a historical transformation, and data captured over a period of years provides a unique window into cross-generational changes in class structure and position. The field methods I used to gather the data are common to cultural anthropology—participant observation, and a raft of other qualitative methods, including a series of interviews with key informants and their families, as well as mapping exercises and quantitative surveys. I have also included work from other researchers' studies that support the present ethnographic study, beginning with the early work of Doug Butterworth (1973), which was based upon his students' research, as well as that completed together by Michael J. Higgins (1972) and Arthur Murphy and Alex Stepick (1991), as well as my own previous work (1990). My personal field research with Colonia Hermosa residents was completed over six fieldwork sessions between the years 1968–1972 and 1996–2000.

In her edited biography of Ruth Benedict, Margaret Mead wrote, "What happens on the growing edges of life is seldom written down at the time. It is lived from day to day in talk, in scraps of comment on the margins of someone else's manuscript, in words spoken on a street corner, or in cadences which lie well below words that are spoken" (1959: xv). This quote reminds me of how it is to experience fieldwork, and of my own intuition that what one learns while doing fieldwork is best described as "scraps," which, when finally pieced together, lead to an understanding of the logic of the social practice under study. Fieldwork is a very personal experience, but it is also based on particular strategic methods. It is both an experiential and a cultural activity. When I first began fieldwork in 1968, my student partner and I were both complete novices. We wandered around the colonia introducing ourselves to residents by asking, "Is this Colonia Hermosa?" The question revealed our naiveté, and some residents were worried that we were the legal owners of the land that they had illegally taken. But, as we were to find, residents were also forgiving and extremely generous. They were not only interested in helping us with our Spanish, but also happy to discuss their lives and their community. During that first summer, our goal was to meet the community and to finish the assigned work (Butterworth 1973).

We returned the following year, 1969, to Colonia Hermosa, this time as residents. It was then that I began my work with unstructured interviews and life histories. During this second period I focused on curing and medical beliefs, and began to look at economic strategies. Although I had set out to investigate both men's and women's lives, the women were so singular, and their lives stood out so vividly, that they came to be the major focus of my work. Thus, again completing a series of unstructured interviews and life histories, I came to study the lives of these women and, through them, their families. As each year passed and we returned, I became friends with many colonia residents. As a matter of fact, returning to the same field site was probably one of the better methodological strategies, as relationships and trust grew deeper over the years.

It was in the third year of my fieldwork that I gave birth to my son in Oaxaca. This event changed everything. This fundamental rite of passage opened new doors, and I was finally accepted as an adult woman. It's important to point out that before then I had not known that I was not considered fully adult. I only became aware of that change after the fact, which is a salutary lesson to any beginning social researcher who thinks that filling in a questionnaire or doing an interview results in scientific data. Such methodological naiveté takes little account of the quality of the information being gathered. Throughout this early period of participant observation, and into the following decades, I continued using the wide tool kit of ethnographic methods, but what is most important, I think, is the process of data selection.

Data as evidence lead inductively to theoretical arguments, arguments that rise from patterns that seem to appear from experience. In turn, these first theoretical arguments provide the building blocks for further studies and can lead to more concrete proposals that sometimes find their way into social policy. In my case, the data selection strategy resulted from a mixture of my own deliberative thinking (thinking through the lens of habitus and field), the context of contemporary anthropological and sociological work, and the self-conscious selection of particular stories and ideas presented to me by my informants. They determined the pathway of our discussions. Thus, the conversations that informants had with me served as markers for what was important to them, and highlighted the concurrence between individual lives and the structural features of the larger society. By "structural features" I do not mean only the economic and political structures of city and the state, but also those aspects of residents' lives that provided the immediate context in which they lived. The contexts in which they located their conversations were sometimes taken from the newspapers, or from their everyday experiences, or from their personal historical narratives and self-identity, and, finally, sometimes from local gossip. When I selected what I eventually used as data, I focused on the common themes and stories that were repeated continuously, and which developed patterns and scripts. Thus the data began to form the outline of my theoretical arguments. The frequent repetitions of certain types of data from informants revealed much about them as individuals and their connection to the larger world.[3] Sometimes central conversational themes or an important event became explanatory devices that unlocked key elements in an individual life, and were referred to time and again. I would always have to pay particular attention when an informant was beginning with a particular story (for instance, the constancy of the Virgin) or why certain suggestions (the slightly suspect role of being someone's mistress or "second wife," as it is euphemistically termed) lurked in the background of conversations. Now and then an important feature of a person's "script" would be an event that they would not discuss or would elide. Such subtextual "moving off target" would signal to me that there was something I needed to investigate and think about more deeply.

In response to the data I gathered and to the experience of my field-work, I have used a practice-theoretical methodology, which has allowed me to mediate subjectivities and economic structures, and which attends closely to the lived practices of the colonia residents.[4]

FIELD, HABITUS, AND CAPITAL

When I first met Colonia Hermosa residents in 1968, they were busy with the process of redefining their economic dispositions so that they would more fully correspond to the structure of the larger society as they understood it, and which itself was an emerging postcolonial capitalist economy. I want to make it clear at the outset that what I describe in the book is not what is termed by other social scientists as *cultural change* or *acculturation*, but a transformation of cultural models and values. This change is one that "takes place only through the mediation of the experience and practice of individuals differently situated with respect to the economic system" (Bourdieu 1979a: 1). Within the *field* of the lives of the urban poor—"field" here taken to mean the space of social interaction, conflict, and competition—the individual is shaped by both the larger societal imperatives, as well as by family history and class habitus.

By "habitus," I refer to Bourdieu's familiar notion of dispositions created by the influence of social structures on individuals. It is in the exchange with history that individuals generate their self-perception and the possibilities that they see for the future (Mahar and Wilkes 2004). Taken together, the field of objective structures and the formation of a personal habitus can be said to have structured the social practice of my informants, and to have helped to transform and generate residents' dispositions toward their futures. The use of these two central concepts, field and habitus, allows us to link class and social space with family, individual dispositions, and personal agency (Mahar 1990, 1992).

As dispositions and future goals changed, Colonia Hermosa residents used what *capitals* (socially valued goods) were at their disposal for strategic use. The following example should help to explain what I mean.

Aída is a colonia woman who insisted on a formal education for her eldest son, Santiago. She lived in the most difficult of circumstances but was resolute that he not leave school in order to work, but instead finish his training as an electrician's apprentice. Aída came from a background of rural poverty, and she had only three years of primary school education. Unlike others in the colonia, Aída opted for the kinds of choices that would provide a better life for her son in the city. She did not rely upon prayer or a relationship with a special saint to change her circumstances, as did many of her colonia contemporaries. Instead, because of the sort of person she was, and because of the influence of her first husband, she held to the promise that an education would make a difference. Aída says that she had a happy life with her first husband,, even though she was his "second wife." This husband had had only a primary school education and was determined that his son would do better. The choice for Aída was made easier because of her son's positive attitude toward school and work. One of Aída's strategies (though perhaps unconscious) was to convert her high symbolic capital, built through her reputation and good works in the colonia, to economic advantage. Her good reputation sustained itself through her decision to live alone without a man, her hard work, her practice of regularly paying her bills, and her role in helping with community projects. All this meant that her neighbors would help her with jobs and credit. In this way, her son could remain in school instead of having to work to help support the family. By 1985, Santiago had become a successful electrician in the city and had moved his mother and two brothers into a better house in a different urban-poor suburb. He also moved his wife and daughter into a different house. Their Colonia Hermosa lot was too small to build additional rooms. The long years during which Aída exchanged her high symbolic capital for credit and struggled to make sure her son completed his education had reaped substantial economic and social rewards.

In order to appreciate the changes in Aída's life, the importance of the economic dimensions of her investment of symbolic capital needs to be emphasized. Bourdieu uses the term *capital* to refer to socially valued goods of various qualities. *Symbolic capital* frequently refers to status, prestige, and social standing or honor—attributes that Aída had in large measure. She was, in fact, rationally, though probably unconsciously, calculating the economics of virtue. In this situation, the symbolic capital of her role as a good mother and a reliable community person was transformed into other types of capital: *cultural capital* (jobs, education, friends, networks) and *economic capital* (income and other financial resources). While the power of symbolic capital was clearly recognized by residents as being important in maintaining social relationships among households, it was unrecognized as contributing to women's positions within and beyond the household. The expectation that women were responsible for family members also allowed them access to their husband's pay, control over their own economic projects, scope to pawn household goods, and access to their children's labor. From the perspective of the larger world of capital, these resources were negligible, but for colonia women they were, and continue to be, crucial.

The general framework of this study hypothesizes that the transformation that took place in the lives of Colonia Hermosa residents with regard to capitalist modernization is associated with a change in lifestyle that can be conceptualized as moving from a more "fully lived" world to a world dominated by economic thought. The use of the concepts of habitus, field, and capital allows us to conceptualize both the personal level of family life and personal agency, and their connection to the outside world. Seen in a dialectical fashion, such interplay necessarily creates a different mode of living and practice from that which migrants experienced in smaller, more homogenized communities. The changes in dispositions or habitus, which are fundamental to changes in class positions, are not only reflective of individual lives, but collectively result from the homogenizing effects of popular culture. The attention in this study to class and personal transformation echoes a general interest in the larger discipline of cultural anthropology, increasingly concerned with the movement of information, symbols, capital, and forms of representation of nonlocal influences (Kearney 1995: 547).

CONCLUSION

In general, people in Colonia Hermosa viewed the key to their success in the city of Oaxaca as having to do with three very basic strategies that they claimed had provided the reasons for migrating from rural villages to the city in the first place: to educate their children, to work hard at whatever job they could find to earn money, and to obtain land titles to the house sites that they had settled. Not only did these practical factors combine to form the basis upon which their lives were built, but they also provided the basis for the common goals upon which the early colonia community was established. At the same time, attitudes, subjectivity, the role of religion and family—all of what I have called "the lyrical voice"—also came through, as well as the practical voice. However, while a subjectivist shift in dispositions has certainly taken place over the generations, there is very little evidence of any substantial changes in class position for many of those involved. Among the twenty-five key families I interviewed (out of the original three hundred families), only half of the generation of children who are now adults can be said to have advanced into the working class, and far fewer into the middle class. Many residents still live lives of desperate poverty and exploitation, a commonplace experience for colonia residents, though routinely misrecognized as such. What is most compelling is the self-identification of one's place in a class-stratified society, and the clear ideological structures behind such reasoning. This process of self-identification separates them from any possibility of seeking revolutionary activity for fundamental political change.

If we are to make sense of colonia residents' strategic pathways, we will need a broad anthropological methodology, using the wide variety of ethnographic tools available to the cultural investigator. And we will need to make use of the theoretical concepts of field, habitus, and capital if we are to grasp how these individual experiences connect to the larger social forces beyond the experience of the individual. This is the path I pursue in the ensuing chapters. In what follows, I set out the stories of individuals who are engaged, up to their neck, we might say, in the struggle for survival in the city in order to unlock the social logic that explains both their individual experiences and the shape of the social structure that surrounds them.

I begin in Chapter 3 with a case study of a representative community woman whom I refer to as Consuelo Alvarez. The trajectory of her life is emblematic of the broader changes in social practices among women in general, who have, according to their perspective, been successful in making the transition from being a poor urban migrant to an urban citizen.[5] In her personal account, the impact of larger social forces is clearly felt, and her life is powerfully constrained by them. As well, the power of her family and class habitus also becomes apparent in a review of the trajectory of her life.

Class habitus can be read through Consuelo's dual use of spirituality and economics as the principal strategies for overcoming her poverty. The dispositions that were engendered from her family become clear through the approaches that Consuelo takes to her life, her identification of self, and how she has structured a successful existence. As you read about Consuelo, keep in mind the connections between economic constraints, class habitus, and family habitus. What is immediately evident is how these personal, class, and societal structures have changed over time (after all, people and societies are not static), and how, at the same time, nothing has changed. For Consuelo to confess, or even to feel, that she is not successful, and that she is not "at home" in the city, would be to admit defeat in the face of ideology and her self-identity. Such ambiguous structures of belief and practice inhabit all of our lives. Implicit in Consuelo's tale is the necessary process of misrecognition, or *méconnaisance*; such ideas enable life to go on in the face of impossible odds, while, simultaneously, the structural integrity of the urban poor is preserved.

CHAPTER 3

CONSUELO'S STORY

CONSUELO LIVES SEPARATELY from her mother on a piece of land that is situated on a rise up from the main road. A piece of the wooden picket fence in front of her house is broken, and she does not have the money to fix it, nor does she want to right now. The house and the land are not in her name, nor in the names of her children. There are three houses on this lot, which is full of medium-sized deciduous trees. It could be a really beautiful setting if the yard was not filled with construction bricks, wash tubs, an assortment of tools, and the like. One of the houses belongs to Consuelo's brother-in-law, a second is rented out to a family whose daughter is her son's *novia* (girlfriend), and the third, where she and her sons live, belongs to her late husband's grandmother. Consuelo's boyfriend, Adan, has paid 1,000 pesos to have her telephone reconnected. She has been seeing him for two years, but does not want to marry him as she likes being treated like a novia. Her house has no light except from a bulb on a wire taken from her brother-in-law's house. She owes more than 2,000 pesos to the electricity board. Apparently the account was in her husband's name and was never changed. The board will now charge her for the past two years to cover the time period that the board neglected to send a bill.

We sit in her living/dining room and look at photograph albums, and then she shows me the two bedrooms and the kitchen. One of the bedrooms is full of her son's electronic disco equipment. She has rather modern living room furniture, and not the usual rough wooden furniture purchased from the local market. This room has two large chairs, one housing a mother cat and her kittens, a couch made of red velvet material that is old and soiled, a large glass cabinet with lots of china knick-knacks, and a TV that does not work on top of the cabinet. One of the walls has a large picture window. Everything is dusty, and the place looks as though no one really lives there, but, of course, they do.

There are many pictures on the wall, including a large photograph of her late husband, Carmelo, as a young man. The floor is tile and marble—rather grand. Yet despite her house and furnishings, Consuelo still seems to be fighting the same battle against material poverty and the "look" of poverty that characterized the life of her mother and father. I feel great compassion for this woman, this friend, who works hard, who is crazy about her sons, but who has made some poor life decisions.

GENDER AND STRATEGY

I have chosen to talk about this particular woman because her life reflects many of the problems and strategies that challenge women in general in Colonia Hermosa. I first met Consuelo in 1969, when she was fifteen. She had just finished primary school and was working at home, helping her mother to care for her five younger siblings. Due to her domestic responsibilities, she did not go on to high school (intermediate or middle school in the United States), nor did she attend a job-training program. Schooling was problematic, not only because she had to help her family, but also because at the time there was no primary school in Colonia Hermosa. This meant that she had to attend school in another colonia—a slight hardship, perhaps, but one that kept her in school past the normal six years of primary grades. In general, from the time she was very young, she has characterized her life as one of hardship and some rare triumphs.

Although I first met the family in 1968, I did not get to know them very well until 1969, when my husband and I lived in a house very close to theirs, just slightly up the hill. Consuelo would hang around our house, curious about what we were doing, what food we were cooking (her favorite food at our place was French toast), and expressed an interest in learning the polite way to use utensils. At the same time, her family kindly adopted us. While they were among the poorest families in the colonia, they were always offering us food, a little bit of whatever they were making. We responded in kind. I remember how, as a newcomer to the task of anthropological fieldwork, I sometimes felt particularly homesick or suffered particularly deeply from culture shock, and I would sit in their cook shack listening to the chatter of the children, and watching Consuelo's mother, María, cook *empanadas*, or make *mole*, or slap out tortillas on the grill. The smell of roasted corn dough was intoxicating, and the rhythmic slap to shape the tortillas was a comfort to me. It was a warm, domestic space in which I always felt safe and welcome. This, of course, is not what Consuelo was looking for in our home. For her, we were something novel; our lives were mysterious, and therefore exciting. We were not stuck in Colonia Hermosa, nor were we living in poverty. To her, we were a symbol of a larger life—one that she imagined to have glamorous possibilities. In this way, we exchanged what we needed personally for what we could give one another. When we left that year, she took our curtains and made dresses.

It is important that I make clear from the beginning that while the material conditions surrounding her might seem daunting to us, Consuelo does not see the world in which she lives as inhospitable. Rather, for her, in her late forties, the world is full of possibilities. She would agree that her life has been difficult, sometimes verging on the desperate, as money and debt seem always to have been an issue. But she does not see this as being an impossible situation, merely a condition for which she has not yet found the right formula or strategy. She is constantly searching for a way out of the poverty that keeps her in continual debt to her late husband's creditors, for resources to meet the electricity bill, and for funds to meet the needs of her two teenage sons.

Consuelo's natal family is a typical example of the changing family structure in the colonia. During the early settlement period, neighbors would help to support one another with food and other essentials. Nowadays, the neighborhood help system is not much used because the children are now adults. More than likely, they live in the same squatter compound as their parents, in much larger houses, or, as in the case of Consuelo's family, they have enlarged the parents' home to the extent that it acts as a gathering place for siblings. In this way, a network of adult siblings has established itself as a support system to replace the larger community, which once worked as a network of household support.

There are several abiding themes that Consuelo's life suggests as I go through her interview tapes, and as I reflect upon our long acquaintanceship and my work in Colonia Hermosa. One of the most powerful impressions that emerge from all of the colonia lives is the permanent condition of economic constraint, which maintains these social aspirants in survival mode. The talent that colonia residents have shown over the years for making something good out of nothing, save a rough plot of land on a hillside, reminds us that the poverty of material circumstances can stultify and misshape the gifts that the poor could have offered to the larger community.

The social habitus of the community, as exemplified in Consuelo's life, operates around a dual logic of spirituality and economics, the lyrical life and the practical life (God's will and hard work). One theme seems to be always and completely tied to the other. Often residents will say to the question of what the future holds for them, "Well, whatever God sends." In this way, while they always hope and work for something better down the road, hope and fate remain locked together.

Consuelo's visions of the future, first encountered thirty years ago, have structured her participation in the fields of work and family life throughout this period. For many colonia inhabitants, the structured dispositions of habitus have shifted decidedly over time. But for her, the ideas that have shaped her strategies have not altered, and in this way she more closely follows the dispositions of her mother than she does her age-mates. Her family habitus and its dispositions are constantly reasserted in the life story that she tells. Consuelo's strategic practice consists of three essential elements that guide her actions. The first element is a devout belief in her Catholic faith, through her worship of the Virgin of Juquila, which involves the daily use of prayer and religious devotion. The second element is a belief in the value of hard work, both at home and outside of the home. The third element is the belief that there is an ameliorative contribution to be expected from marriage, which has led to two marital experiences. Recently a fourth strategy has been added, and that is the hope that her sons will offer support to her as she ages. This mirrors the experience of her mother. For Consuelo, this latest strategy has not yet been tested.

STRATEGY ONE: PRAYER LIFE

Like many people in the colonia, Consuelo, as well as her mother, have relied for many years on the power of the ritual of prayer. Their special patroness is the Virgin of Juquila, who is associated with the coast of Oaxaca. The town of Juquila lies on the road between Puerto Escondido and the city of Oaxaca. The ritual that pilgrims follow is to promise a series of visits to the Virgin in exchange for her help in their lives. This is a regional belief reflecting Consuelo's mother's rural origins in the surrounding coastal countryside of Oaxaca. Their belief is coupled with a particular practice: consistent pilgrimages to the Virgin's church in Juquila, which helps them to prepare for their future needs. Generally the family asks for help with money matters, children's health, and jobs for their futures. This belief-based strategy characterized most of the households that I worked with in Colonia Hermosa. María, Consuelo's mother, relied on the Virgin for maintaining her family. When something went wrong, it was María who took responsibility, saying that she had not been properly attentive to the Virgin, or that she had broken a promise. Some years ago her eldest daughter died in childbirth at sixteen years of age. Her death was caused by an overdose by the anesthesiologist, but instead of holding the doctor accountable, María confessed that she had broken a promise to the Virgin by not making a pilgrimage to her site on the coast. This, she said, was why her daughter died, so she, not the doctor, was accountable for the death.

Of her own belief in the Virgin, Consuelo says: "Well, for us, at least for me, as you know, we were really poor, and I had to work to get ahead, and to help my family. . . . I still prayed to the Virgin. My mother still asked the Virgin for help. And the Virgin is responsible for all our luck." While Consuelo continues to use the ritual of daily prayer, she rarely participates in pilgrimages now, and prayer itself has dwindled in significance in her daily practice of putting a life together. When she does pray, she has shifted her emphasis toward prayers devoted to her siblings and her children, who she hopes will help her. Thus, while the prayerful life persists, the nature, intensity, and the quality of her spiritual life has changed.

STRATEGY TWO: WORK AND JOB PREPARATION

Consuelo's responsibility for her parents' family, as well as her willingness to work at an early age, both at home and in town, was an early familial strategy used to help her siblings continue with their schooling.[1] It was also a strategy used to bring goods into her parents' home, and it was a typical strategy followed by young women in the colonia. Consuelo worked to transform the home from a one-room shack with no amenities to a modest, two-room concrete house with some modern conveniences. As well, she helped her siblings transform their futures by enabling them to attend school past the primary grades. For Consuelo, hard work was also necessary to "get ahead." Because further education was not a possibility for her, Consuelo spent no time on planning how to train for a career or a technical job. So, like others in the colonia, Consuelo used her network of friends to secure a job—in her case, at a pharmacy—and then stayed with that job for years, building up her skills.

In parallel, since leaving primary school, she had been working with her mother at home and cooking for the family. Her mother worked by taking in laundry and cooking food to sell on the street. They also traveled to the coast, where they sold food and any goods they could bring from the central Oaxacan market. From these elaborate sets of strategies, Consuelo and her mother hoped to find basic economic security, even though, on closer examination, several of these enterprises actually cost the family money, requiring an initial outlay of capital that was more than what was earned. Of her work outside the home, Consuelo said:

> Since I was the eldest, I started work at a very young age at the pharmacy. I didn't go to high school. Neither did Leticia [the sister next in line]. We had to work. My parents were very poor, and what they earned wasn't enough, there were so many of us. Even though my mother worked washing clothes and making tamales and tortillas, it just wasn't enough. So I started to work at a very young age in the pharmacy. I helped first on the counter, and then I learned how to give injections. I got a salary each week, and I learned the formulas to make the preparations for people: for stomachache, for sore shoulders, for rheumatism, diarrhea, and coughs. They sold herbs as well. My mother and I would buy some of these and go to the coast and sell them. I would ask for a few days and we'd go off. We'd do a lot of traveling and selling in the small ranchos where there weren't doctors. We would prepare little packages of herbs, pomades, and little bottles of medicine and sell them all over. This money was to help our family.
>
> Since I was working, I began by buying them a stove and then a refrigerator. We then began to buy materials to make a room. . . . I bought clothes for the children [her siblings], and gave them money for their "recreation." I gave money to my parents so the children could go to school, and I also gave them money for food. My mother took care of Victor [Consuelo's first child]. When I had a vacation, we went off to the coast to sell things; all medicines and tablets and things on sale that we would buy in Oaxaca, like shampoo, perfume, cream, oil, and other valuable items. I told my mother that this was much better than washing clothes or making food to sell on the street.
>
> We also saved some money, and with that money we bought the materials so my father could build my little house below my mother's

on their plot of land. Some time before, when my father was building my house, he asked me for a loan. When he couldn't pay it back, he gave me the house—all the labor and whatever materials he might have bought himself. Later I bought the paint and all the other things. Then, Leticia left primary school, and she began to work in a car parts store as a sales girl, and then joined me at the pharmacy. Later we were both representatives for a business selling wines and spirits. She earned really well. She also helped with the family and we both earned. We helped Dante and Efran to continue studying. Marisol and Moises were still in primary school, but later Marisol trained as a nurse and married a country doctor. Moises trained in regional tourist dancing and met his wife. He now paints and sells little wooden animals for tourist shops, but he is not very successful. The other two boys went to high school too. Efran was really studious and became a military officer. He lives in Mexico City. He just loved school. Anyone could go to secondary school—you just have to pay to register the children. Another thing that really helped us was that my father got a good job in construction. He had helped to build one of the ISSTE [federal] hospitals, and he was recommended to them. So the children didn't need to leave school to help.

Like others in the colonia, Consuelo consistently voiced the belief that success in life depended upon having a good job, and that in order to secure a good job, one must have at least secondary schooling.[2] Nonetheless, this is clearly not what she did. So, while she claims that education is a key component of success in the workplace, neither she nor her parents were able to secure that training for her or for her next sister, Leticia. But they did help secure it for other family members. In her own work life, she has moved from her job at the pharmacy to selling beauty products door-to-door. Because she must buy the products before her clients buy from her, her business often runs at a loss. Sometimes they change their minds, and she must borrow money to continue.[3]

Victor, Consuelo's eldest child by her first husband, lived with his father as her second husband was abusive. Victor is now an engineer. Consuelo has two boys, aged sixteen and eighteen, by her second husband. One of them has fathered a child and lives now and then with his in-laws. He left high school and currently works for a soda pop factory to pay for an apprenticeship as an office worker. The second boy works in a furniture factory but is finishing high school, hoping to attend a technical school to train for a job.[4] For the future, she says that she is counting on her sons to help her live into old age as she becomes too tired to work outside of the home. She hopes that they will have good jobs, and that they will inherit their grandmother's home, where they currently live, and where she hopes to open a little restaurant in her living room and kitchen.

While Consuelo would disagree, I see her work life as one that closely resembles her mother's, and that remains very far from the pattern followed by her better-schooled siblings. Mother worked at home as well as cooking food to sell on the street. Consuelo sometimes cooks at home to sell food from her home to local workers and students, as does her sister Leticia. Mother worked selling food and picking up laundry door-to-door in Oaxaca. Consuelo sells beauty products door-to-door. Mother worked selling goods on the coast of Oaxaca. Consuelo continues this pattern, although the nature of the merchandise has changed. A clear difference between the women lies in the style exhibited in their two homes with regard to furniture and appliances. Consuelo has red plastic living room furniture, a small china cabinet with figurines, and other goods typical of working-class urban households, as opposed to the more basic wooden tables and chairs of her parents' home. Her boys have electronic equipment for their music, while her mother had only a radio and a TV. And Consuelo's clothes have a much more urban look to them than her mother's. María continued to wear simple cotton or nylon dresses, as well as her black *rebozo*, in a more rural style. Consuelo's house, while very limited in size and quality, is a step up from her mother's house, which still reflects the rural look of their original house site.

STRATEGY THREE: MARRIAGE

Like other women from the colonia in her age cohort, Consuelo has tried to use marriage as a way to climb out of the desperate poverty of her family. In following this strategy, she has been decidedly unsuccessful, though others have had better luck. In her family alone, two of her sisters have married well, one to a country doctor and the youngest sibling to a lawyer with a village practice.[5] Her sister Leticia married a first-class bus driver, which is considered to be a good job, providing a steady income and medical care through the Social Security doctors. Her three brothers also "married up": one to the daughter of an orchardist; one, the military officer, to a lower-middle-class woman who now assumes a very middle-class lifestyle; and the third to a woman whose father taught him the business of making the small wooden animal figurines sold in Oaxacan tourist shops.[6] This pattern of marriage between subproletariat and working-class with lower middle-class people is reflected throughout the colonia.

Consuelo became pregnant with her first child at seventeen. I remember when she and her mother told me, while they were at my house having some French toast. Recently Consuelo had not been especially close to me, and I had felt that there was something wrong. I remember worrying that I had perhaps done something to upset them. Finally, the story came out. Consuelo seemed embarrassed, as did her mother, that she had to get married. I remember being puzzled by this, as it did not matter in the least to me. I struggled to get them to understand that, for me anyway, this was not something shameful. The problem, however, was with the boy's family, and Consuelo was very upset at the possibility that the marriage might not take place at all. The bridegroom came from one of the colonia families considered "wealthy." Not only did they have a substantial cement house (a step up from the crude wooden, one-room shack of Consuelo's family), with a collection of furniture that included beds (instead of the *petates* that her family used), but also the father was a rural schoolteacher. Although such teachers need only complete grades 1–12, the job ensured that the family enjoyed a monthly paycheck from the federal government, as well as medical coverage through the federal health program, ISSTE. Her fiancé, Roberto, was also expected to become a schoolteacher.

Roberto's parents did not approve of Consuelo's family because of their poverty, their lack of education, their lack of volunteered labor for the colonia, and the father's habit of drinking all weekend. They felt strongly that their son was marrying beneath him. Even though Consuelo was in love with Roberto, part of this love was tied to the possibility of her future—one in which she was married to a schoolteacher and living a life free of pressing financial need. As it turned out, that was a romantic fantasy; the marriage did not succeed either economically or emotionally. Consuelo, like most women in the colonia, continued to be responsible for taking care of herself and her child, as well as any household obligations. In addition, she continued to have a major responsibility for bringing money into the household:

> I worked at the pharmacy before and after I married Roberto. When I had Victor, I worked until I was four months pregnant. Then I stopped work, and when we had Victor, neither of us were working, and we had to buy milk for Victor. We couldn't ask for everything from his

father, so I started working again. Then, after that, from there, I left
the first pharmacy and was hired for a better wage at another pharmacy. They paid me more because I already knew how to prepare the
formulas, and I prepared them there. I also helped a lot around the
house because we were no longer living in Roberto's parents' house. By
then Roberto had gone to Mexico City to work in one of his brother's
workshops. I went to my parents, who were still very poor. It is for this
reason that when Roberto and I separated, he didn't want to fight for
anything, because he knew that everything was mine. I put together
the money and saved it in the bank.

While separated from Consuelo for two years, Roberto became involved with another woman, which led to their divorce. Some time
later, but still unmarried, Roberto earned a high school diploma and
began to teach at a rural school. He continued his education until
he graduated with a professional degree in civil engineering. His and
Consuelo's son, Victor, followed him into this profession, and, in fact,
Roberto now teaches at the technical institute where Victor completed
his education.

In the early 1980s Consuelo met and married her second husband,
Carmelo, who worked as a driver for a large first-class bus line in
Oaxaca. This job was considered to be a very good position and provided good, secure wages. Consuelo says, "With Carmelo, I was completely in love." Unfortunately, Carmelo was an alcoholic and became
very abusive to her and to the children when he was drunk.

Consuelo says:

Carmelo drank because he liked it, but not because he was mad or jeal-
ous. We didn't have this type of problem. At first he told me not to go
out and work, and that I should stay at home. But he wasn't working,
and I wondered how were we to do this? He'd go off with his friends,
and I had to do the house and food for his mother. But we didn't have
jobs. And one day I said, "What are we doing? We are both fit and well,
not sick. . . . You don't want to work? Well, don't work. But I do." And
you could tell that the neighbors would say that we didn't have any
money, that we were lazy; it embarrassed me a lot. And it hurt me that
we were eating at his mother's house and at my mother's house. Well
that's okay for now and then, but not all the time. We needed money! I
started to go to the coast with my mother, so my mother gave me a lot
of support to start working again.

As indicated in this account, Carmelo was unable to keep a steady job because of his addiction, so again Consuelo became responsible for keeping the house (Carmelo's grandmother's house) and the family together. In addition to her work at home, she worked as a representative for a liquor company, setting up displays in various city stores, and she also continued to sell goods privately on the coast. While Consuelo was working, Carmelo would take her money and spend it to go out with his friends. They both borrowed money: Consuelo to begin new business ventures, which never worked, and Carmelo to gamble. In the late 1990s, Carmelo died of hepatitis and liver failure.

By 2000 Consuelo was still deeply in debt, mostly, she says, to her husband's creditors. Her little house that her father built on her parents' property was sold to her sister, Marisol, and the money was used to pay off some of the debt. It is important to remember that she now has no property of her own, and because of this, she is in a more vulnerable position than her mother was. In a sense, she has bet on the strategies of marriage and hard work, but at this juncture in her life, neither strategy has been successful.

In the earliest days of my work in Oaxaca, collective support was routine, even though nobody spoke of it as an aspiration, or a common good, or a social capital. During those early days of living in the colonia, Consuelo's mother and her neighbors relied on one another for loans of food and for help with their children. Now, however, this situation has changed for every family in my study. People do not rely on their neighbors, but rather on their kin, especially their siblings, since they are the ones who support the family home and who usually live together on their parents' original land, or compound. Community, more broadly conceived, has been replaced by family. For individuals like Consuelo, however, there is the continual necessity of the extended family support system. Consuelo has never consciously conceived that the use of family support might be a strategy for survival, but she uses it continually to this day. In her negotiations with the electricity board, she goes to her brother-in-law, the country lawyer, for help; for medicine, to her sister; and for money, food, or company, she goes to her sisters and an older brother. What is interesting in her "use" of her siblings and their resources is that she knows that they are not close friends, and that, because of her relationship to them, she occupies a lower position because she has very little symbolic capital. She says, "Leticia doesn't have a lot of confidence in me because of my life with Carmelo. I will talk with my youngest sister [Aurelia], and sometimes I go to her house to do laundry, and she will buy a lot of food and feed me and the boys. Sometimes my brother in the army will give me advice or talk to me about things." Her sisters and brothers acknowledge the early sacrifices that Consuelo made for their collective good, but they disagree with her lifestyle—first, because she married a drunk (making a strategic mistake), and second, because she herself is interested in parties and drinking, and left her children too often with their mother. With regard to her second husband's family, Consuelo often talks about the family house she needs to survive. Unless Consuelo can claim her now deceased mother's house (which all the siblings use as a meeting place), she will continue to live on the charity of her dead husband's family.

During one of my last days in Oaxaca, Consuelo and I met for a final conversation. As the day and evening progressed, I met another side of Consuelo (the one her siblings do not like) as well as her boyfriend, Adan. I include my field notes from that day because it illuminates Consuelo's present life and reveals, for students, a small part of the relationship between anthropologist and informant, which is a kind of friendship.

A DINNER WITH CONSUELO:
THURSDAY, THE 15TH — FIELD NOTES

Today was eventful. Consuelo came to visit me at Sam's place, the bed and breakfast where I am staying (Sam is a retired American expatriate who lives in Oaxaca). As always, whenever I am in Oaxaca, she likes to visit me wherever I'm staying: hotel, pension, or house. I like to visit her at her house too, though we mostly see one another in town, or at her mother's house—even now, although her mother is dead, we often meet there. Our visits are not always for "work," so we sometimes spend the day visiting the graveyard or having a coffee in the zócalo and buying flowers. I think we have a type of friendship, but I am fully aware that there is also a "veil" which covers the discrepancy between our lives, and which helps us to misrecognize her need for whatever money and gifts I give her, and my need of her as an informant. Anyway, I like her and that's that. We completed an interview this afternoon, which I think is good.

Consuelo is enchanted by Sam's place. Well, so am I! She is also taken with Sam himself and his apparent wealth. She has a beer after the interview, and we sit in the patio and chat. Sam is cooking dinner and he invites her to stay. She goes home, changes and comes back. (She's wearing a tight, black dress, heels, and looks really nice.) When she comes back, she has another beer and then another. We eat. She and Sam drink wine. And then they consume another two liters of beer. Then they have three more glasses of wine. They are using regular water glasses, so they are really drinking a lot. Finally, the two are completely drunk, and begin to sound like stereotypical drunks; one in English and one in Spanish. Sam tells me that at night when the 'boys' help him to bed he has them lay down—outside of the bed and fully clothed and hugs them and says "thank you" to them for their work. They cry!!! (Oh dear!! This is so strange.) Consuelo tells Sam that if they were "together" . . . that with her he would never need Viagra! This was in response to something he said or something she thought she heard! Anyway, he's flirting too. Meanwhile it's raining cats and dogs. I am wondering how I am going to get Consuelo home in a taxi. I am beginning to feel desperate—everything is just so out-of-my-hands!!! Then, some other guests report a water leak in their rooms and ask to be released from their contract. Sam is furious, besides being rather drunk, and he takes this personally. He finds them another hotel and goes to bed with chest pains. In the meantime, I must restrain Consuelo not to go into his room. She calls her son for a second time that evening. She is maudlin; she tells her son how much she loves him, and how she loved his father, and that she'll be home soon in a taxi. Her son speaks to me and says not to put her into a taxi, as she would be taken advantage of; that he was coming to get her. Later on, at the same moment that the other guests (all women) leave for their new hotel, Consuelo's boyfriend, Adan, arrives. He is a very nice-looking, very tall, rather stern middle-aged man. I can't tell if he's angry or not, or perhaps just concerned. He wears a frown on his face. I am glad that Sam is nowhere in sight, and that with all the women leaving, he'll think that this was a North American women's party. I think that he could be seriously angry and I'm feeling nervous. Actually I have had the giggles all night. Finally, everybody is gone. Quite an evening. . . .

CONCLUSION

When I asked how she envisioned the next two decades of her life (she was forty-eight when we had this particular conversation), Consuelo said,

Well, continue working as much as I can. I think that I will try to do up the house and put a little business there. A restaurant or *taquería* so that when I'm older I can work there. Doing as much as I can. If you are sick, what do you do? What hospital? I don't go anywhere but to a private doctor or the general hospital (Consuelo has no health coverage). My brother who is in the army can help me; one of my sons has social security in his job. . . . Maybe Victor will help me . . . or someone! Perhaps Victor can.

As I mentioned in the previous chapter, I asked my informants to tell me how they viewed success, and how one was to become successful. Their responses seemed always cut from the same mold, and closely resemble the dispositions expressed by Consuelo, if not the actual conditions of her life. Generalizing from the comments of Colonia Hermosa residents, one comes to realize that their "theory of success" is that if one is to survive and thrive in the world of capitalist modernization and globalized culture, there are strategies which one must cultivate, and a community wisdom which one must accept and invite into one's life. For my informants these were clear elements of the urban habitus: the necessity of schooling and job preparation, living a good Christian life through hard work, family responsibility, and the love of God. The main focus for each of them was on the achievements of the individual, even though, as is clear in the stories that follow, success has routinely been built with the help of neighbors and family—that is, through collective help. The opportunities, they say, are there: one must only "aprovecharlos," or take advantage of them. This, I think, is their testament to the power of the state and the market, which drew the rural poor, and these families in particular, to Oaxaca some thirty years ago. When discussing her brother Moises, Consuelo blames his failure to succeed in the business world on his lack of initiative and his laziness. She characterizes herself as successful—simply temporarily "out of luck."

Consuelo's tale demonstrates that individual identities and social practices are constructed through the dialectic between personal dispositions and the external reality of objective structures. For Consuelo, or any colonia resident, to confess that they are not successful and that they do not feel "at home" in the city would be to admit stark defeat in the face of the ideology of the individual that they have taken up. Such ambiguous structures of belief and practice inhabit all of our lives. While my informants often reiterated their belief that they are successful, and "truly citizens," we all are aware that those faced with limited resources, twelve-hour workdays, and limited education will not be able to truly share in such citizenship. And while some individual families "succeed" and others "fail," at the same time the structural integrity of the urban poor is preserved. The broad truth of the story of the rural settlers is that some of them can become, by extraordinary effort, successful members of the urban working class with some attendant security. For many others, however, such as Consuelo, a life in the subproletariat remains their fate: self-employment for little economic gain, no health care, no security, and little real citizenship or entitlement.

Méconnaissance—misrecognizing the objective structure or real divisions of the social order (Bordieu 1972: 163)—makes survival possible. As with all of us, misrecognizing the truth of the social world—which is generally, in society, the universe of the undiscussed, "the undisputed 'real'"—enables life to go on (Bourdieu 1972: 168). The social logic of late capital in Oaxaca finds a place for squatters in meeting the needs of the marketplace—as sellers on the street, workers in the stores and in the tourist industry, and low-cost laborers. Social fields are not only places of struggle; they are sites where communities seek to change the logic of the field, even as they struggle for success within it. But for this generation, and a person such as Consuelo at least, the urgent need to survive saps them of the strength to fight the larger struggle for a change in the nature of the social logic itself. No messianic revolution is at hand. Subjective expectations face up against history, and history, as Fredric Jameson (1998) tells us, is what hurts. Until the hurt is eased, the people I worked with will fight to enter a new logic of exploitation, the logic of the working class in a society where unions have little power, and the dominant will of globalization drives a hard bargain. This they will count as success, and under these conditions, survival is indeed success, and their lives represent an extraordinary achievement against all the odds.

In the following chapters I explore their successes within the social fields of community, family, and employment, focusing on the strategies that the other colonia residents have used to maximize their social and economic capital.

CHAPTER 4

PLACE AND IDENTITY

MATERIAL CONDITIONS AND SOCIAL IDENTITY are closely inter-twined. This chapter narrates the establishment of place and the for-mation of urban identity among the citizens of Colonia Hermosa. The narratives you will read are a testament to this community's deter-mination and their endless work, and an intimation of their hopes and dreams—for themselves and for their community. Landscape and identity are always intertwined, and the environment of the colonia is no exception. Through their construction of houses and the develop-ment of the large compounds that came to contain them over the years, residents reveal their material successes, the fruits of their immedi-ate labor, which are direct and measurable evidence of their progress. These houses embody a central part of the social, material, and sym-bolic capital of the new residents.

A NEW PLACE

My introduction to Colonia Hermosa was very simple. In 1968 I was a member of a group of graduate students from the University of Illinois who traveled to Mexico, along with our academic adviser, Doug Butter-worth, to investigate the squatter settlements of Oaxaca. After driving close to 2,000 miles from Champaign-Urbana, we began our first sum-mer of fieldwork in Oaxaca. When we arrived at the colonia, it was a very hot morning in June. After parking on the side of a broad, dirt road, we walked over to a nearby construction site. The workers were all men, and all wore cotton shirts with their sleeves rolled up, and cotton pants in varying states of wear and tear; some of the men wore western or rancho-styled hats, with the cords hanging off the back brim. Every-one was working. Surrounding them were piles of dirt, bricks, bags of cement, picks, shovels, and an assortment of smaller tools. The lasting sense I have of that first morning in the colonia is one of extreme heat, the smell of dust mixed with the odor of garbage, the sound of radios blaring out advertisements along with the music from ranchero and mariachi bands, and the very strong sensation of my being quite out of place: this was my first field site, and I was the only female in the group. Doug went over to the men and introduced himself.

The leader, or spokesperson, of the group stepped forward, shook hands with Doug, and introduced himself as Enrique Guzmán, the president of the colonia's Mesa Directiva. He explained that he and his colleagues had recently completed the first classroom building of a new school, and that they were now constructing a bathroom. The building and the bathroom facilities were to be opened by the local PRI candidate for governor; they seemed very proud of what they had accomplished. Butterworth then explained our presence, as students who wanted to learn more about Oaxaca and to "practice our Spanish." We often invoked this as an explanation and as a way into a community. This also positioned us as students vis-à-vis colonia residents. He asked if one or two of us could work in the colonia. Permission was granted, introductions given all around, and we left to find another colonia, where a third member of our student group could work. Michael Higgins and I thus began our first period of summer fieldwork, fieldwork that was to stretch into years, within Colonia Hermosa.

At that time we were funded by a grant that Professor Butterworth and other professors had received. The earliest work from this research resulted in a collection of essays edited by Robert E. Scott and published as *Latin American Modernization Problems: Case Studies in the Crises of Change* (1973). From the beginning, it was clear that the colonia defied any previous stereotype developed by government agencies as being illustrative of a generalized urban crisis, which was the commonly held belief about squatter settlements in the broad sense. Colonia Hermosa, however, was different. In 1968, with about three hundred households, it was the largest settlement of its kind in Oaxaca, as well as being the most complex and the wealthiest. In an early article (Butterworth 1973), the colonia was characterized as being a poor urban suburb, not a squatter settlement, despite the fact that most of the residents were squatters.

After we had obtained permission from the head of the Mesa Directiva to work in the colonia, Michael Higgins and I began our work. Of course, this was not a one-sided process, and many colonia residents had their own thoughts about us. Many thought that we were the legal owners of the land, just back from Los Angeles, or, alternatively, that we were Protestant missionaries. The first rumor died of its own accord, but it was only when I became a *comadre*,[1] and residents understood that I was Catholic, that the missionary idea evaporated, and all of their homes were opened to us. The fact that I was married but did not have children was a worry to some of the women in Hermosa. Because I was a Catholic, they were certain that I did not use birth control, so they set about arranging to "warm" my womb, an event that never took place because the magical qualities of the gusty, hot summer winds made it too dangerous to proceed. I accepted this excuse, but I also thought at the time that the woman who was to conduct the ritual felt a little shy—just as I did.

COLONIA FAMILIES: STAKING A CLAIM

Over the years, from 1968 until 1974, I would routinely ask new colonia residents why they had come to the city of Oaxaca, and to Colonia Hermosa in particular. The answers were routinely the same—that they migrated for what they termed "a better life." To them, this phrase concretely meant several things: a better education for their children, better-paid jobs for themselves, and access to city services such as health care. The fact that residents have struggled year by year to improve their homes by continuously rebuilding and enlarging them is one of the more obvious manifestations of their anticipation of a positive future.

An even greater testament to their investment in their future was the work that residents contributed early on to the development of their own households and their community, and to the city, by providing basic services. They worked together on common community goals, so that even before its incorporation into the city of Oaxaca, Colonia Hermosa was well developed, organized, and had a stable population. As well, residents were already incorporated into the city structure by means of their use of local markets, employment, health care, and by where they chose to go for their leisure, such as walking around the main square, the zócalo. Hard work and tenacity had enabled them to carve out a place and form a new identity in the city—and thereby to survive.

When they first arrived in the colonia to build their houses and their lives, the new residents were uniformly young, usually in their late teens and early twenties (86 percent), and most had small children. More than half of the workers were either unskilled or had only basic manual skills. Some found jobs in the city doing the same type of work they had done before, such as driving buses, plumbing, or working for the military. For everyone the construction of a "future" and the measure by which they judged occupations was not so much by income, but by the degree of job stability. For this reason, a man such as Arturo, who used to sell popsicles on the street before he came to Hermosa, chose to continue this job when he moved to the colonia. Like others, he felt there was no reason to change just because he had to take a bus ride into the city. For the same reason, Aída's eldest son was desperate to stay in school in order to train as an electrician, even when the family moved to the colonia. Job stability in itself was and still is a career aspiration. Being young, and coming from central city rented apartments or from rural villages, colonos had the most to gain by owning their land through living in a squatter settlement, thus freeing themselves from monthly rental obligations.

Thus very soon the house site itself became a spatial metaphor for their situated practices and future aspirations. The practice of cutting sites out of the hillsides and constructing houses provided migrants with an objective space that not only conformed to the establishment of community, but also provided a location that was to be transformed into part of the city structure. At the beginning of Colonia Hermosa's development, one of the links of solidarity between residents was their mutual poverty, their shared lack of basic services, such as water and electricity, and their tenuous claim to their house sites—all of which brought them together in communal work.

By the late 1980s, consumer goods were becoming available to some colonia residents, and in subtle ways, forms of stratification were clearly developing. This division most clearly evolved between those who were in steady, paid work and those who were not. For those who had become successful in the city, the transformation from their shantytown homes in a squatter settlement to houses that later became part of a city suburb, and the change from mattresses and petates[2] on the floor to the purchase and use of beds, allowed residents to begin to live their success. The material circumstances around them directly signified their individual success. And the sensibility that shaped their evolving sense of identity moved away from any consideration of community welfare or group feeling, as in the past, toward a future imagined in private terms. This change in sensibility and dispositions is critical in order to understand their later chronicles of success.

What follows are the accounts of three families and their trajectories over thirty years: how they have, in their own words, "moved up" in the world, as manifested by their new forms of personal property and the emergence of an associated habitus of new dispositions. Colonia Hermosa residents feel quite straightforwardly that changes in house types and material acquisitions are a reflection of their success. An important part of their narratives reflects how families mustered the resources necessary to create their footholds in the city. The family homes in the early days were extremely humble, as the photograph in Chapter 1 (Figure 1.2) makes clear. What is also evident are the differences, by the late 1990s, in the layout of the colonia, the size and quality of people's homes, and the growth in their ownership of material goods (Figure 1.3). The changes within the colonia in terms of economic, symbolic, and cultural capital, and the shifts in community identity were very evident by 1995, moving as they did from community goals to individual ones.

As the community of the colonia began to become formally incorporated into the broader structure of the city, the original familial households, basic one- or two-room shacks, were developed into larger houses and often compounds with multiple houses. Families have built larger compounds or have sold their original land and house in order to move to another, more compatible colonia. Others have simply moved to larger homes, using the financial help of their grown children, but have held on to their earlier house sites. The original settlers do not easily let go of their land, even if they move to live elsewhere. Too much was *invested* here—in every meaning of the word.

The awarding of legal title to their land from the city was a critical step that provided the security upon which families could plan a future. Equally significant was the family strategy. Families grew in wealth and security through their collective or extended family help, and not as individual, single-family households. As the example from Consuelo's life demonstrates, everyone in the extended family was somehow helped by others in the family. Nowadays help is always limited to one's connections to the natal family. As the narratives illustrate, affinal[3] help is connected to natal families only by way of one's married sons and daughters. By this I mean that outside the nuclear family, there were no friendship ties to other affinal connections that helped to support the original parents and natal households. This is in stark contrast to residents' earlier experiences, when they initially set up households in the colonia. At that time friendship networks were a much more decisive factor in family achievements.

By the 1990s, some of the residents' children had benefited from government-sponsored schemes that had helped them to buy a house or secure a mortgage. Similar to receiving title to their land, these programs provided a way of giving younger residents a base upon which to build a place in the city through their own home ownership.

Finally, it is important to appreciate that until this newest generation grew to adulthood, most of their parents did not use banks or have anything to do with other formal financial or social institutions. This has been a major generational transformation of real significance, and it suggests not just a new stage in the process of institutional incorporation, but a shift in identity that is profound.

MARÍA'S FAMILY

When I first met María, she could usually be found leaning over her washing tubs, energetically working and talking, laughing and barking out orders to her children. María came from the coastal region of Oaxaca and met her husband there when he was working as a laborer. Although she was not an overly large person, she gave the impression of being substantial because of her ebullient personality. Except when it would fall about her, she wore her black hair plaited and caught around her head. Her face was large, generous, and friendly. María and her husband, Alfredo, a sparse, mustachioed man, were in their late thirties when I first met them. They had lived with his mother in town when they initially came to Oaxaca, but then had moved to the colonia. Alfredo worked as a poorly paid day laborer who picked up construction jobs by standing on the corner of the downtown square, the zócalo. Their plot of land in the colonia lay in the upper half of the first section, and they lived there with seven of their eight children in a two-roomed house made of wattle and daub (later of cement and brick), with a pounded dirt floor and a tarpaper roof. They stored their belongings in cardboard boxes or hung them on the walls using nails. Their sleeping arrangements consisted of two shared beds, an assortment of petates, and mats made from cardboard boxes. Prominent in the first room was a table used as an altar. This housed María's collection of pictures and other objects dedicated to a variety of saints, but especially to the Virgin of Juquila, as well as a glass jar of flowers and a few votive candles.

FIGURE 4.1. María (*right*) with her daughters Consuelo (*center*) and Leticia, 1969

For María, this altar and her cookhouse were the center of the household, and the iconic markers of her family.

In both rooms of the house, as well as in the yard, their radios, like those of their neighbors, played all day long. This was the one commodity that everyone in Colonia Hermosa owned. Next to the house was a separate cookhouse with a pounded dirt floor in which were set out the traditional tools—a *mano, metate,* and *comal*[4]—as well as a two-burner kerosene stove and a few, very short wooden chairs and stools. María used one of the stools when she cooked. The outhouse was situated behind the house. For water, they had tapped into a supply pipe that ran down the hill from a well, and thus had a water tap in their yard. Also in the yard, which was not large and was cut out of the hillside, they grew a few fruit trees, some stalks of corn, and an assortment of potted plants, and they raised a small number of chickens and turkeys.

María was born in a mestizo village on the coast of Oaxaca near the town of Puerto Angel. Her original household consisted of her father and mother, her maternal grandmother, her older brother, and herself. It was a small family. She finished first grade and then left school to help with chores at home. She would help with shopping, laundry, and making tortillas, which her mother and grandmother sold at the local market. She also cared for the few pigs and chickens that her parents owned, and she gathered wild fruit and greens for the family to eat. Her brother remained in school, and later, when she was nine or ten years old, he left the village to work in the city of Monterrey, where he lived until his death. Because he was several years older, María was not close to him, and he did not figure as an important person in her family's life. However, when I first met her, they did exchange letters at least once a year. By the time she was fifteen, the household included only María and her mother, as by then both her father and grandmother were dead. María was working full-time as a seamstress, sewing for the local women. She became pregnant, and because there was no male head of household, the father moved into María's house and began a free union marriage with her. Apparently this husband was a drunkard, and after a year he left the house and broke off all contact with the family. María then supported the household by sewing, while her mother cared for the little girl and sold tortillas and other homemade foods at the market.

After four years, María met Alfredo, who had come from the city of Oaxaca to the coast looking for work as a mason. Alfredo offered financial support as a husband in a free union marriage, and María became pregnant with their first child. They decided to move the entire household to Puerto Angel, a rather large coastal village, where Alfredo was working. At this time María gave up her full-time occupation as a seamstress and joined her mother selling at the market or doing odd jobs for other households, again sewing and doing laundry. During their years in Puerto Angel, five of María and Alberto's eight children were born, none of them more than two years apart. It was also then that María's mother died. By 1964 the family had moved to Alfredo's natal city of Oaxaca. They lived in a small inner-city apartment, along with Alfredo's mother. María did not get along with her mother-in-law, who, she said, was demanding and short-tempered with the children. Within a year, the family had heard the radio advertisements about the land in Colonia Hermosa, and they had decided to move.

If, in the late 1960s and early 1970s, there had existed a social ladder categorizing the economic and symbolic capital of each colonia family, María and Alfredo would have been located somewhere toward the bottom of the hierarchy. They did not always have cash, but they did have some appliances, such as a sewing machine and a radio, which they used to pawn regularly to get cash, and they almost always picked up work, Alfredo continuing to find sporadic work as a mason, and María by selling food and doing laundry. However, in the arena of symbolic capital, which includes community respect, the family would have been rated low, except, perhaps, by their immediate neighbors. They were considered to be a large, noisy, messy, and argumentative family, with a father who was known for his Sunday drinking bouts. Their clothes were often mended and thin with wear. The children were rather unkempt, and the teeth of the youngest girl were black from her lack of good food and milk. Furthermore, they demonstrated little loyalty to the colonia as a community group. They did not participate in the tequio[5] or with the Mesa Directiva, saying, by way of justification, that those neighbors who did get involved "are all in it for their own personal interests." As well, they only occasionally participated in school functions, and they shopped in the center of town rather than in the colonia. Apart from a few women neighbors, their compadre ties were entirely with city families. But still, some of the neighbors would visit and gossip with María, and I believe she enjoyed their companionship even though, between ourselves in conversation, she might dismiss them.

AÍDA AND HER FAMILY

Aída came to Colonia Hermosa with her second husband, Carlos, and their three children in 1965. She was born and raised near the Oaxacan state border in a mestizo village in the state of Puebla. She was brought up in a *matrifocal*[6] household, supported by her mother and cared for by her grandmother. During her first fourteen years, Aída completed primary school (through grade 6) and was taught basic skills such as cooking, sewing, and cleaning. When her grandmother died, Aída was fourteen, and at that time her mother gave her to a wealthy family to work as a maid. For this work she received no payment except room and board; however, she did say that her mother received a regular stipend for her labor. She also confided that the husband in the house sexually abused her. She remained in the household for a year, and then, at fifteen, she met her first husband, a free union arrangement. She became pregnant and they began to live together. The man was about twenty-five years old, from Oaxaca, with a steady income as a truck driver. After their son, Santiago, was born, they moved from Puebla to the city of Oaxaca and set up their own household in a downtown city apartment.

Aída's husband also had a first wife and family, so she would have been his second wife—not an unusual situation. As he was a truck driver whose route took him between Puebla and Oaxaca, it is not in-

FIGURE 4.2. Aída and her youngest sons, Gustavo (*left*) and Alejandro, 1969

conceivable that, like other men with two households, he regularly visited both wives and their children. What is interesting is that in all the years that I have known Aída, we have never spoken at length about this husband's first wife, although she spent many hours telling me stories about the perfidy of her second husband, who left her for another woman. Perhaps because in this case she *was* the second wife, and, because of her sainted reputation in Colonia Hermosa (upon which was based her symbolic capital), she felt more comfortable glossing over this particular facet of her life.

While growing up, Aída had felt close to her grandmother, although she had always felt that her own mother had disliked her. Later in her life, this was shown to be clearly the case in dramatic fashion: in 1968, her mother claimed a woman's dead body to be that of Aída. She brought the body back to the village, announced Aída's death, and held a funeral and a *novena* for her. Symbolically, this was tantamount to burying her daughter alive and finishing all ties with her. The next year Aída returned to Puebla seeking a copy of her oldest son's birth certificate. On the way, she stopped in the village to visit her mother. The local people, who thought they had buried her the previous year, were astonished to see her. In the 1990s, Aída and her mother finally reconciled. This came about through the assistance of her older brother, who had never figured in her young life, but as he grew old and was abandoned by his wife and daughters, he sought the friendship of his sister. Aída's son Santiago helped to pay for the medical care that the grandmother needed before she died. Aída explains her mother's attitude toward her when she was a young girl by saying that she had had a very hard life, that her mother worked the fields like any man, and therefore, in "the deepest parts of her," became more like a man. Thus, as Aída explained to me, her mother's working life had had a kind of magical impact on her physical and emotional state, making her tough and mean like a man rather than a caring, nurturing woman. This was the way Aída accounted for her mother's cruelty. It also tells us so very much about Aída's notion of gender roles and behaviors.

In reminiscing about her past, Aída remembers her first husband as being very energetic and ambitious. She said that he was anxious to raise their standard of living. As she spoke about their life together, it was clear to me that she adored him. She remembers him trying to teach Santiago to read before kindergarten. She looks upon this time of her life as one in which she felt secure and upwardly mobile. Eventually they began to collect many material possessions, such as radios, a blender, cooking utensils, beds, lamps, and a sewing machine. After five years of marriage, Aída told me, her husband had suddenly died. This was in 1969. In a later interview, in 1999, she simply said that he "went away."[7] In order to sustain herself and Santiago, she began to sew for local market vendors.

Aída's second husband, Carlos, worked as a highway construction worker for the Department of Public Works. When they met and began living together in Aída's apartment, she hoped that they would have the same secure life that she had experienced with her first husband.

Her decision to live with him was based on the promise of economic security. Within the first three years of their de facto marriage, Aída gave birth to two children, a year and a half apart, Gustavo and Alejandro. When the two little ones were born, the entire family moved to the colonia and built their house on the side of a small ravine. It was a large wooden, two-room structure, with plenty of land around it to expand. In it were all of Aída's possessions from her first marriage. Although Carlos did have a steady income, he did not take the kind of care and responsibility for the household as did Aída's first husband. According to Aída and her neighbors, he spent his money on drink and on other women, so that even though he did have a good working-class income plus health benefits, he did not support the family well. Thus, during their marriage Aída continued to work outside the home to sustain the household.

In 1967 Carlos abandoned the family entirely and left the city with another woman to live and work in a Oaxacan coastal town. Now, with three children to care for, Aída was again left on her own. Worse was to come. Soon after this period, during the rainy season, a heavy storm loosened the foundations of the house directly above her. The consequence was that it fell during the night and completely destroyed her own home, nearly killing her youngest son. The effect was catastrophic. The home, all of her carefully planned and thoughtfully collected possessions—in short, all of her economic calculation and strategy to that point—had come to nothing.

Very few items were salvageable. Even the land itself disappeared down the gully. With the help of her neighbors, she moved her family to a higher, narrower piece of land. Her son Santiago and a local compadre built a one-room wattle and daub structure. But this was going back to the beginning. Two beds, a few pots and pans, a table and some chairs were all that was left of the earlier life and the two marriages. Even her sewing machine, her way of making a living, was lost. In 1968, Aída's de facto husband, Carlos, was still working for the Department of Public Works. At the urging of her compadre, Aída went to the *ministro público* (district attorney) and attached her husband's wages on the basis that he had claimed his two sons by her as his legal dependents. As a result of her action, she received 200 pesos a month. With this money, along with the money she raised making tortillas and doing laundry, she was able to sustain her household. Unlike other colonia children, her son Santiago never stopped attending school in order to work full-time. Although he worked part-time to help meet his own expenses and received a government-sponsored scholarship, his money was never counted toward the household budget. Santiago's education and a career as an electrician continued to be a family goal for their mutual advancement.

When I first met Aída in 1968, she was head of one of the poorest households in the colonia. However, she was also regarded highly by other residents. She was replete with symbolic capital. It was unusual in the colonia for the poorest people to be the most respected, and so Aída was, and remained throughout her life, special in this way.[8] I argue that there are at least two reasons that account for this anomaly. The first is that after her second husband left her, Aída did not become friendly with any other man, nor did she become involved in another de facto marriage. Rather, she maintained a high moral status. She completely devoted herself to her children and denied herself any life apart from them. As the ideology of the Virgin (the self-sacrificing mother) is strong in Mexico, Aída was characterized by community members as coming close to that ideal type. A second reason for such respect is that she routinely participated in community events, so she was seen to be generous with whatever help she could offer, despite her poverty. Aída was particularly active on the school committee, she had many friends in her area, she traded with the local store, and she always paid her debts at the store within the week. Hence, Aída was viewed as a hard worker, a good mother, and a good neighbor. In this "saintly" life, Aída thus embodied the highest form of symbolic capital: the altruistic, self-sacrificing model of traditional virtue. In exchange, she obtained credit, work, and gifts from her neighbors.

Of course, Aída's new home revealed her true poverty. The shack was constructed from thin wood shingles and had a tarpaper roof and a pounded dirt floor. Aída and her two youngest sons shared one small double bed. Santiago slept on a petate. The room was furnished with a rough wooden table and two chairs purchased on time-payments from a door-to-door salesman. All goods were kept in cardboard boxes or under the bed. There was no electricity at first, so they used a kerosene lamp. Later the house was fitted with one wire taken from the main electric wire along the colonia path. There was no cook shack nor outhouse. Aída cooked outside in the small yard on an open fire, using the traditional comal, and when it rained, she cooked inside on her one-burner kerosene stove. The narrow patch of land behind the wall of the house and the hillside from which the house site was cut were used as the family's latrine. This arrangement was not unusual in Colonia

Hermosa. In the dry and hot season, only the torrential afternoon rains cleansed the dust from the paths, which was mixed with drying human and animal feces.

While Aída only had a few dresses and a black rebozo, or shawl, her son Santiago always took the trouble to dress as well as possible in the usual uniform of urban poor schoolchildren: a white, short-sleeved shirt, dark trousers (not jeans), a belt, and black shoes (not tennis shoes or sneakers). Her other two sons, who were still very young, usually wore only shorts or underpants with a T-shirt, and sometimes shoes. Their long pants were kept for visits to town. The house was cleaned and swept each day; food was put away in plastic containers or bags, and showers were to be had every so often in the local Colonia Hermosa baths for one peso.

ISABEL AND ARTURO

When I first met Isabel and Arturo, they lived high up on the colonia hillside, on a large lot, with Isabel's mother and young brother, her two sisters, and their children. There were three separate homes built on the lot. Isabel was the only sister with a husband, and at the time they had three children. Arturo's brother and his six children also lived on the lot in Arturo and Isabel's wattle and daub house.

Isabel and her sisters were born and raised in a highland Zapotec village. Their father still had land in their village, although he lived in the center of the city. Arturo and his brother were born and raised in a Mazatec village.[9]

Some years before, Isabel's father had inherited a small parcel of land in his village through his father. Although their family was not among the poorest families in the village, neither were they considered wealthy, and the land was not enough to sustain both them and their father's brother's family, who had also inherited the land.[10] Migration to urban cities is a popular alternative to village life for those within this mid-economic level of village life (Butterworth 1973), and this family elected to follow that trend. Isabel's father was the first family member to make his way to Oaxaca to find work in the market as a laborer, carrying heavy goods, though he did not give up use rights to his land. He began living in the center of town with his compadres,[11] which is another way that rural folk found initial shelter in Oaxaca. Later, his wife, Elena, and their three girls, Isabel, Teresa, and Rosa, as well as his young son, Eduardo, joined him. They all lived in the center town apartment. Soon after this, the father left the family and took up resi-

FIGURE 4.3. Isabel and Arturo's first house in Colonia Hermosa, 1969

dence in another downtown unit. He had decided that he no longer wanted to live with his wife, although he did want to see his children.

When their father left, the sisters were teenagers, and they worked with their mother to support themselves and their brother. All four of the women worked for a well-to-do Oaxacan lawyer's family doing laundry, cleaning, cooking, and tending their children. During the late 1960s and early 1970s, Isabel was no longer working for the family, but Elena and Rosa continued to do so. Teresa also no longer worked for the family, but was still connected to them through giving birth to two children fathered by the young, married son. Although he did not visit her in the colonia, he was the sole support of Teresa and his children. Teresa continually fantasized that he would live with her and take her as his second wife. This did not happen. By 1999, Teresa had given birth to eight children with different fathers. She currently works as a maid in a local Oaxacan hotel.

Isabel met Arturo when she was sixteen. He had migrated from his Mazatec village to Oaxaca, where he worked as a street vendor selling for his compadres, who owned a popsicle factory. When Isabel became pregnant, Arturo moved into her family's apartment. In 1966 Arturo and Isabel moved to the colonia. The couple set up house in the second section, high up on the side of the hill. They cleared a section of ground

FIGURE 4.4. Isabel with two of her children and her sister Rosa, 1969

and built a one-room bamboo and mud structure for sleeping, and an outside lean-to for cooking. Later, Arturo replaced the house with one made of adobe bricks constructed by his brother and his eldest son. When I first met the family, their furniture was much like María's and Aída's. There were two crude wooden tables and some chairs, a cook shack made of wattle and daub, containing a comal, mano, and metate, and a kerosene stove. The family shared a double bed with their youngest children, while the older children slept on petates on the pounded dirt floor. Isabel also had a treadle sewing machine that she used to make clothes to sell at the market. All of their belongings were kept in wooden or cardboard boxes.[12]

Next to this house and the cooking area, another smaller room was constructed to accommodate relatives, such as Arturo's brother and six children when they came to Oaxaca. Neither house was equipped with electricity or water. For light they used a kerosene lamp. Water was drawn from a well close by. Soon after this household was established, Isabel's mother, sisters, and young brother moved to the colonia. Arturo built a bamboo, mud, and tarpaper house, along with a cook shack to accommodate them. The house was dug well into the hillside, so that one wall of the interior was part of the hill. Later, Arturo built another single-room house a little lower on the hillside; it was another mud and tarpaper room for Rosa and her children. From 1968 to 1973 Rosa gave birth to three children, each by a different father. She continued to work for the lawyer's family and would take her children to work with her.

In the early period of my research, Arturo's brother had left, so this entire domestic unit consisted of three households. They helped one another with child care, marketing, cooking, and fiesta days, but they did not exchange money. If they did borrow from each other, they always repaid in kind almost immediately. With respect to finances, these families lived separately. In other respects, they functioned as a unit, and were bound by close ties of kinship, friendship, and cooperation.

In terms of the larger colonia community, Isabel, Arturo, and their family are interesting because they were, from 1968 to 1974, considered to be of almost no consequence to anyone in the colonia, even though they were staunch members of the tequio group, and compadres with officers in the Mesa Directiva. When they discussed the development of the colonia, they gave the impression that they were highly integrated into this core political group, yet others, including some of their compadres, rarely acknowledged them. In fact, their compadres from the Mesa Directiva denied them the right to buy a stall in a new market that was established by colonia residents, for a time, directly across the highway.

Without any kind of power, social or economic, this family clearly played the client role in any patron-client relationship. This, I believe, was due to what others would define as their "Indian" dispositions, which led them to employ exotic (exotic to the community, that is) strategies which were not understood or accepted by the largely mestizo community, and which allowed others to categorize them as being "just indios."[13] Having been raised in indigenous villages, their first language was not Spanish. Furthermore, the indigenous residents tended to assume a low profile, an almost "cap-in-hand" attitude when presented with a public mestizo gathering. This feeling that indios are naturally inferior was extremely prevalent in the colonia and, indeed, in the city itself. Upon first meeting, most of my informants would deny any indigenous background because indios were said to be ignorant of civilized ways. Since Isabel, Arturo, and their family were so obviously indigenous, this may account for them having been treated as though they were invisible. This condition, however, has changed dramatically, and in the 1990s, I found them to have a new sense of confidence and entitlement, and they were very proud about how they had managed in the city.

TWENTY YEARS LATER: THE LATE 1990S

MARÍA'S FAMILY

In June 1996 I returned to Oaxaca for the first time in twenty years. Everything was different. I found my way up to María's compound with some difficulty, as the vegetation was overgrown, and the houses had grown much larger. Everyone had more than one TV, and there were electricity lines all up and down the streets and paths. It was not clear to me whether they were all legal electrical hookups, or if residents continued to use illegal wiring.

Twenty-two years ago, María's eldest son died in a bus accident,[14] and now her husband had been dead for seventeen years. María was much thinner than I had ever seen her, and she was suffering from diabetes.[15] Her youngest son, Moises, was there. Apparently he often lives with his mother when he is in town. He was painting the little wooden figurines that are sold in tourist shops. He calls himself an artisan, and he is married with one son. His wife and son are at her father's home in a local village. It was Moises's father-in-law who helped him into the business of wooden *animalitos,* one of the popular tourist items that are crafted in the village.

María's children helped construct the compound, which nowadays seems to be the household style of choice in Colonia Hermosa. They have constructed a series of bedrooms, each connected to the next by a common wall, with two rooms opening out onto a common patio. Her daughter, Marisol, her husband, and their two children were using one of the bedrooms while they fixed up Consuelo's little house, which she had recently sold to them. In this room they had their own furniture, which consisted of a double bed, a single bed, a chest of drawers, and a TV. Another room was used for storage and was filled with boxes and a number of household items. There are cement floors throughout, and they are painted dark green and dark blue.

FIGURE 4.5. María (*center*), her daughters Leticia (*left*) and Consuelo, and her grandson (Leticia's son), 1995

There is also an open-air kitchen, with a roof but only three walls. Here, María keeps two wooden tables, several wooden chairs, a refrigerator, and two gas stoves fueled by propane tanks delivered to the colonia from local vendors. Two of the bedrooms open out into this kitchen area. One is María's, and it is equipped with a TV, a double bed, and a huge altar commemorating various saints. Another room had belonged to a third son, Dante, who is now on the coast working as a surveyor, and who also helps his father-in-law with the family orchards. He is married and has four children. Like María's son who lives in Mexico City and is a career military officer, he helped to pay for María's medical care in the city some time ago, but as of 1996 he had not sent any money to her for a while. As with many colonia families now, aging parents seem to rely on money from their children to cover some of their expenses. At the time I was first there, María worked part-time selling tamales in the city and selling soda pop and small snacks in her open-air kitchen, which doubles as a small store. In the past María was renowned for her *mole poblano*,[16] which colonia residents and her compadres in the city used to purchase from her. She was also well known for her delicious mole tamales, wrapped Oaxacan-style in banana leaves.

Despite having an indoor kitchen, María often used her old outside cooking area, where she cooked with her charcoal *anafre* (stove) as well as a comal for cooking homemade tortillas. Thus she continued to cook using the older familiar styles and utensils. All of her daughters cook inside their houses in kitchens fitted out with propane gas stoves.

As mentioned in Chapter 3, Consuelo is María's daughter, and at the time of my visit she had just sold her old two-room cement house, below María's, to her sister, Marisol, and her husband. This sister is one of the two youngest daughters, both of whom were able to complete primary and secondary school. She then went on to finish technical school training as a nurse. Her husband is a doctor from rural Oaxaca who hopes to open a practice in the colonia. María cares for their two daughters while they work.

María's youngest daughter, Aurelia, does not work and lives in a large village just outside of Oaxaca with her husband, a village lawyer, and her young son. They live on her husband's parents' property in a large house made of concrete blocks, with a concrete floor, and which is structured along the lines of an American suburban house, with a living room, a dining room, a kitchen, hallway, and bedrooms. Aurelia's son, along with Marisol's eldest daughter, attends a small, private kindergarten located in Colonia Hermosa. During my visit, Aurelia arrived after having collected the children from school. She was bringing them, along with some groceries, to their grandmother María's house. When I last saw Aurelia, she was very small, and her baby teeth were black with cavities due to a poor diet: a surfeit of soda pop and diluted Nestle canned milk, which colonia residents often fed their children because they could not afford enough canned or fresh milk. Because of her poor heath, I had often wondered what would become of her. Nowadays Aurelia is the tallest of the sisters, and very beautiful. At her mother's house she visits with the family, cooks food, washes a small load of clothes for her mother, and then leaves for home. On the day I visited, Aurelia invited her sister Consuelo and me to her home for comida, their large midday meal, later that week.

Finally, Leticia, Consuelo's third sister, came through the door along with her husband and son. Like Consuelo, she did not finish school, but worked as a liquor representative in a variety of city stores. Leticia is married to a man who works as a bus driver, and who had been good friends with Consuelo's husband. The three stop to chat but do not stop to eat.

Leticia's house is nearby, and she is anxious for me to see it and to admire it. She takes me up to her house, which is around the corner from María and Marisol's houses. It sits high up on a rise and is accessible only by very steep concrete steps. Leticia proudly shows off their small red car, and her house, which is structured around a patio and consists of a living room, dining room, three bedrooms, a kitchen, an indoor bathroom, and a room for their washing machine. The family was able to buy their house through a government loan program that was organized to help the working poor. Like her mother's house, Leticia's is furnished with Oaxacan wooden market furniture, but it also contains a media center for tapes and CDS, and two televisions. While we talk, her son is occupied with his Play Station games. Like her mother's house, the floors are painted, though they need sweeping as trash is usually thrown on the floor and then swept up later in the day or the following morning.

I asked Leticia about her family and her own life trajectory. We talked first about María's devotion to the Virgin of Juquila and how she fervently believes that the Virgin would take care of the future, and then we discussed her notion of how one should plan for the future and what may come. Leticia said:

Well, more than anything I am very religious, I believe in the Virgin of Juquila. She has helped me a lot. I have a promise—my husband and I—we went to see the Virgin even though he is from Oaxaca and not the coast. When we got together we spoke a lot about this. At the beginning I could not have children, almost for two years. So, we went to Juquila to give us a child and made a promise. I became pregnant that year. We made a promise that we would never leave the Virgin. Always every year we ask for something, but we work very hard too. One year I asked for this house. You see, we were paying rent, and paying rent, and moving all over, even to Etla, then to Colonia Hermosa to Consuelo's little house. My mother rented it to me for two years. Then we bought here and have been here for six years. I asked for a car and it cost us a lot of sacrifices too; you just don't ask for something. It is necessary to work really hard to save. I also asked for other things—it's a lot of work for me to have any money, but that's the way in which one progresses. The Virgin helps us work hard through our faith. This year we have asked for a baby, and for it to arrive healthy and strong. Because we are both getting older—he is thirty-nine and I am forty. I have a doctor, but there could be a problem. We also will thank the Virgin because everything is going well with us. Health, jobs, and sometimes we even go away to the beach for a vacation!

It is clear to me that each sister was anxious to have me appreciate and admire their houses, their families, and the good fortune that they each felt they had enjoyed. Their beginning in the colonia was desperate. Food was in short supply; everyone was forced to live in one bedroom, to use petates for bedding on the pounded dirt floor, to use cardboard boxes for their clothes and other possessions, and to use an outhouse. I realized anew how they had suffered from the humiliations of material poverty, and with them I felt glad that, in their eyes, they had succeeded in their lives. Nowadays food is not scarce, their homes are large and equipped with a sewer connection that allows them to have an old-fashioned pull flush toilet. Also, each house is equipped with a stereo and CD player, a television (or two), a gas stove, and a refrigerator. The fact that they are connected to the globalized marketplace through the media, and through their young children's music and style preferences, is critical to their feeling that they are "part of the world," and that they have a place in Oaxacan society. No longer on the margins, they feel that they are full players in the developing economy and the evolving self-identity of Mexico.

Owning a working gas stove and a refrigerator means that María's two daughters, Consuelo and Leticia, are able to follow their mother's path by having an in-home restaurant. By the year 2000, only Leticia had taken up this option, but as mentioned in Chapter 3, Consuelo is considering opening a small restaurant in her living room. Also, Leticia rents their extra bedroom to two students who study at the nearby technology institute.

AÍDA AND HER SONS

When I returned to Oaxaca in 1996, I found that Aída had sold her house and her small parcel of land in the colonia, and had moved across the city to another colonia. Her eldest son, Santiago, owned a house and land there, but lived elsewhere. Aída was now sharing the house with her youngest son, Alejandro, his wife, Nelli, and two young boys (aged six and nine). A few years later, in 2000, Nelli left Alejandro and the children. Aída took charge of caring for the children despite her poor health, which continued to decline. When she was very ill, she lived with Santiago and his family until he and his wife divorced. In 2007 Aída died at age sixty-nine from ill health connected to her problems with diabetes and her heart.

Sometimes, Alejandro and his family would move to a second house that he had bought with Gustavo, the third brother. This occurred now and then when Nelli could no longer stand being around her mother-in-law, Aída. Then Aída would continue to be taken care of, and, in turn, care for Gustavo and his family. While Aída was respected and liked in Colonia Hermosa, she was viewed as dictatorial and moralistic by both Alejandro's and Gustavo's wives—especially by Nelli, because Alejandro was always tied to his mother by the invisible cord of Aída's gentle but persistent demands and the guilt that Alejandro felt if he did not agree with her wishes. Generally the wives would instigate the move out of Aída's house, as Aída can be judgmental and controlling. They and their families alternated living with Aída in her compound and up higher on the same hill on their own property.

Aída decided to sell her colonia house because it was empty (she had already moved) and was being used by local teenagers for drugs; "a real house of sin," as Aída described it. I asked Aída about Colonia Hermosa, and how it had grown since 1968. She answered:

It is much better than before, because the streets are better, they have pavement, they have telephones, light, water, and it is cleaner. . . . We live here because Santiago bought this land with a house of one room made of adobe. This room where we are now didn't exist. And he constructed part of the house. . . . Well, then Alicia, his wife, through her work, got a house [a three-bedroom condominium in town] through a lottery from work [which provided help with a loan and down payment]. So we came here. I said to Santiago that we didn't need to come here, because we already had our house in the colonia, but I saw that living was easier here. The hill wasn't so high to climb, and it was easy to find a bus to town. The piece of land we had there was very small, and the house was in very bad condition because we needed a lot of money to redo it. Here, there was room to put a car, there was water, light, a bathroom, and the *molino*[17] is close [where she can buy the corn masa to make tortillas]. I have lived here fourteen years. I lived in the colonia for twenty years or so.[18]

Here in this new neighborhood people are equal. The land from the colonia where I lived I sold to a teacher and his wife, who sell clothes in the mercado. Now the section is very different because they have the money. Many people who were there have now died. And, since so many older residents have sold . . . well, there are a lot of new people, and it is no longer the same.

FIGURE 4.6. The author with Aída and her children outside her house in Colonia Hermosa, 1969

FIGURE 4.7. Aída's house in her new neighborhood, 1999

I asked Aída to discuss Colonia Hermosa further. "Do you remember that there was a Mesa Directiva? Do you remember Guzmán?"

Yes, I remember an argument with the other people who bought land from the developer, the teacher. They stayed with their land. They only had a piece of paper of propriedad [ownership]. Not a title. But this paper came from an office. I went to live in the colonia when Santiago's father was no longer around. There, I started living with the father of my two youngest sons. We bought our land from someone who I think took hold of the land when it was only land, no houses; some people only took one piece and others took several; and they had more to sell. Really, there were fights, and there were deaths when the developer was sent to jail with his wife. Also, Guzmán had several pieces of land that he sold. He had seven, I think. This occasioned many fights. There was envy among his compadres who worked on the Mesa Directiva. Then, there was the new market where not just any-one could join. People had to buy in, in order to sell their goods. But today, there is perhaps not so much envy, since most of those people have done very well.

But, for example, Don Enrique [Guzmán] took advantage of a lot of people to better himself. He was a radio announcer, and now he has a hotel right on the highway on his mother's old property. This is the highest he went, but he did very well getting money from wherever he could. And he sold the lots, and who knows now how many he still has. Maybe [he owns] only where he lives, and where his sister lives. Then he had a warehouse for Conasupo [a government-based food cooperative that no longer exists in the colonia]. I don't know if this is still his or not. I think that Superagua [a local water-bottling plant] is his still because his children are working there.

Aída's son Alejandro also had his own story about the move from the colonia to their new location. He explained:

My mother sold the land in the colonia about thirteen years ago. A little bit after, we left the colonia and came to live here. I wanted to go back and stay in Colonia Hermosa with Nelli, but my mother was always worried that I was going to leave her, since I had always been the one at home, the one always spending more time with her. So with this money from the colonia my mother said, "Look—take this money, 2,000 to 3,000 pesos—this is from the land that your father left us."

Somehow between the two of them, years ago, they had bought it. So anyway she gave half to me, and half to Gustavo, my other brother. Santiago, my eldest brother, always wanted us to have it [the money]. So I had about a thousand pesos. My mother told me, "Go put it in the bank," but I wanted to spend it. And a neighbor told me, "Have you seen that they are selling *terrenos* [plots of land] in colonia G.? You should go to see them. They are selling cheap and they're pretty. So, one day in the middle of the week I happened to see my neighbor again. She said, "Haven't you seen the terrenos yet? They're going fast." And so I said to my mother, "Have you found out who owns the land, who is selling it?" and then we went to see it and bought. It cost 2,000 pesos. So then I had to pay each month 250 pesos until it was paid.

From 1995 until 2000, both Alejandro and Gustavo helped to pay for this particular parcel of land. They also built a set of rooms. During the late 1990s they were in and out of the workforce. Finally, in 1999 they obtained regular work delivering bottled water for a local company. Between 2001 and 2003, Alejandro made two trips to the United States and worked in the fields in Tennessee and Virginia.

Until his recent divorce, Aída's eldest son, Santiago, lived in the condominium that had been purchased through his wife, Alicia. Because she worked as a nurse for the Ministry of Transport, she was able to acquire funds for the house through a state project. Alicia is also from Colonia Hermosa, and she works as a transport nurse checking the health of first-class bus drivers. Generally she checks for alcohol and drug use (exactly the sort of check that removed Consuelo's husband, Carmelo, from work). Santiago works for the federal government as an electrical engineer in a local office. He was also very active in union activities. By 2000 he was in his early forties and had four children who all attended private school. Santiago expects them all to complete a university education.

When I first arrived at Aída's house in 1996 after such a long absence, we sat in the kitchen, a cement block room with a long window along one side. The room held a propane gas stove and a large wooden table, which my then-husband, Michael, and I had purchased for them at the central market in 1969, along with some chairs. The room was lit by one bulb hanging down from the ceiling. Like María, Aída continued to use her charcoal anafre as well as her comal, both which were outside in the patio area. The patio was also the place where she kept her dog tethered, and where she had her caged birds and plants. We sat in the dining room and she served me a cup of Nescafé with sugar; no one else joined me in a coffee. What was immediately obvious to me was that there was very little food in the kitchen, and nothing cooking for their comida. We discussed life as they now experienced it. At the moment, work and money were very scarce, with both Alejandro and Gustavo only finding part-time work as laborers.

After my coffee we moved to another room, also made of cement blocks and a cement floor, and which also was lit by one light bulb hanging from the middle of the ceiling. Along one side of the room, which was about eight by ten, there was a refrigerator and some shelving strewn with CD disks, music tapes, plus a tape and a CD player. In the middle of the room was a wooden table, again of unfinished pine, and four or five matching chairs. Here, we sat and looked at pictures. It was in this way that she revealed her family's lives over the past years to me: a series of family photos of ritual events such as weddings, baptisms, and school fetes. Like María's daughters, Aída and her son were very keen to show me how they had come up in the world, knowing that I had been an observer of their most desperately poor lives in the colonia—their one-room shack with a pounded-dirt floor, and the ground in the back of the house sufficing as a toilet.

In their new compound, they were proud to show me that not only did they have more than just the one bedroom, but enough beds: Alejandro and his wife used the original adobe room as a bedroom for themselves and their two boys. In it there were three beds, a television, a chest of drawers and a large wardrobe. In Aída's bedroom she had her bed, a television, a sewing machine, and a small altar with her saints and candles. Finally, as in María's new compound, there was one empty concrete room filled with building supplies, hoses, and boxes full of various items. This was their storeroom. In the front yard, over to the left, was their outhouse: a toilet that can be flushed with a bucket of water is for them a substantial step up.

ISABEL AND ARTURO'S FAMILY

In June 1996, I arranged a meeting with my compadres, Isabel and Arturo. Like the other colonia families, they had not seen me for twenty years. Their son Emilio picked me up from my room in the city and brought me to their compound in a new colonia that lies next to Colonia Hermosa. Emilio sells filters for machines and cars, and drives his own VW Bug. He, his wife, and their son live next door to

FIGURE 4.8. Arturo, his daughter-in-law Adelina and her daughter Carmita, and Flor, Arturo and Isabel's daughter, in front of their new compound, 1996

his parents in her parents' compound. The wife's family is also from Colonia Hermosa, but except for special occasions, such as a birthday party, the families do not come together. Like Aída's family, Arturo and Isabel moved from their original site in Colonia Hermosa to a new colonia. However, instead of selling their old land and house, they gave it to their eldest son, Tomás, and his family. There, in the old colonia, Arturo still has a small, one-room house for himself, and in the yard he keeps his pig, some turkeys, and a small *milpa* (a piece of land where he grows a few stalks of corn). Everyone tells him to sell the land, but he says that he left his *fuerza* (strength) there: all the time and work he gave to building his adobe home (including each adobe brick) and garden. He often walks over just to sit outside in the yard, or in the small adobe room he has built for himself and furnished with a bed and a radio. Tomás's wife, however, does not appreciate these visits and prefers to leave the premises when he arrives.

Because they were the first of my old informants that I visited, it was my first trip down the improved Pan-American Highway, which now has four lanes. We passed a park situated on the site of the original Colonia Hermosa market and continued on past a series of poor urban suburbs covering the hillsides.

Even after so many years, Isabel looked just the same as always, and we spent a few minutes just looking at one another and recalling how, over one summer, she cared for my children while they lived in Oaxaca with their father. Also at the compound were Arturo and his brother, conversing in Mazatec. None of the children have learned either the Zapotec of Isabel's village or the Mazatec of Arturo's home. Their material and family successes resulted from two basic but new circumstances. First, they had their new business, one that Arturo and Isabel now own, making the popsicles that are sold on the street. Second, their grown children were contributing to the collective well-being through both financial support and by living close by or with their parents. Their change in material circumstances had also resulted in a change in their social standing in the community. The family had been making regular visits to the villages of their parents each year, and although the children were not taught their parents' native languages, they still have some interest in the rural areas and their personal history. And, in this new colonia, with the economic help and the social confidence of their children to lean on, Arturo and Isabel engage in the Christmas *posadas*[19] with some twenty-five people and host a large party. No longer did their faces betray shame at being indigenous migrants dismissed by others as "indios."

An adobe brick wall surrounds their compound. The buildings themselves are constructed of adobe and concrete. As one enters the compound, the shower stall and toilet are on the left. Water is obtained from the city pipes, and warmed with a small, wood-fueled heater. The toilet is of the old-fashioned chain-pull variety. Across the patio area are two bed/sitting rooms connected to one another by a doorway.

Isabel and Arturo sleep on a double bed in one of the rooms. Their daughter, Flor, at that time twenty-eight, was sleeping on a camp bed next to her parents. Flor had completed her primary and secondary education, and even her certification to become a rural schoolteacher. When she applied for a job, however, the authorities wanted to send her off into the far rural reaches of Oaxaca, where she would have had to walk, as she says, "half a day, and where there was no electricity." She declined the chance to work and was spending her days at home cooking, cleaning, ironing, and helping her brother's mother-in-law take care of his children. His wife was attending school, working toward certification in computer technology. What Flor really enjoys is her nightlife, spent in the downtown clubs with her friends.

Isabel and Arturo's room was painted white, and the walls were decorated here and there with religious pictures above an altar and a few family pictures. One large window was decorated with floral-patterned cotton curtains. A large television sat on the bureau, covered by a large, floral dust cloth. A second bureau was covered by a mass of washing waiting to be ironed. Isabel's sewing machine was also stored in this room.

The room next to them was being used by their son José, his wife, Adelina, and their three children: two nine-year-old boys (twins) and a two-year-old girl. The room was furnished with a double bed and three cots for the children. There was also a wardrobe and a bureau, which was covered by family clothes and other belongings. Obviously the space was overcrowded, and plans were afoot to construct a new house for Adelina and José on a piece of land next door. Adelina had decided against having any more children, and had a tubal ligation. She is the only woman among all of the female residents I spoke to who took this step in order not to have children. The usual mode of contraception being used was to take injections every three to six months, instead of birth control pills.[20]

Adelina had worked previously as a waitress and says that she met José "on the street," as she had left her home and family on the coast to find work in Oaxaca. She says that she completed only a few years of primary schooling, and that at the restaurant where she worked as a cook and a waitress, they never asked for proof that she had finished school. Now, she says, employers expect everyone to have their primary and secondary papers, so her children must finish school.

I asked her what she hoped for her children, and she replied that first, she hoped her daughter would not go off with the first man she meets (as Adelina herself did) and that her sons would finish school and have a "better life," with stable employment and a house of their own. She was then planning to stay at home with her two-year-old until the child would be old enough for school.

As she cooked lunch at the stove, Adelina said that secretly she would like to go to the United States, but she is worried about immigration problems. Her husband, José, has already worked in the United States and now works with his mother in their popsicle business. She says that "everyone they know" has gone to the North as *mojados* (illegal immigrants without papers). José used to send money every fifteen days (some of which helped his parents with their business),[21] and when he returned, he would bring clothes and other gifts. While the marriage seems to be stable, Isabel confided to me that her son, José, is ten years younger than Adelina, and that he wants to take other women as lovers. She has argued against this, but it was never clear to me whether or not he was unfaithful, except that his mother thought he was. Adelina never mentioned this problem. Like his wife and his sister, José longs to return to the United States to work for a time, but as of 2000 he was still in Oaxaca, running the popsicle business with his mother. (In fact, during the political upheaval in 2006 and 2007 the popsicle business did extremely well from the patronage of the downtown police and demonstrators.)

Next to their bedrooms, and making an L shape against them, is a kitchen furnished with a propane gas stove. The oven is used to store napkins and other objects. There is also a refrigerator, a washing machine, and a table and chairs. Water comes from the bathroom faucet, which is hooked up to a hose. The kitchens may be newer, but there was still the familiar scene of plastic tablecloths, plastic glasses, the thick, white porcelain cups for coffee, the water glass that held sugar, the jar of Nescafé, the cheap metal spoons, and the irksome flies. There was also the familiar and comforting aromas of food: tortillas and the sautéed tomatoes and onions before the rice was added.

At the far end of the kitchen an additional room had been built, and a third son, Domingo, and his new bride were living there. Domingo's wife, Elena, is from Chiapas, but her mother and sister now live in Oaxaca, where she met Domingo. Her relatives make their home across the pathway from her house in Arturo and Isabel's compound. Thus what they have constructed is a compound that lies next to one son, and in which their daughter and two other sons plus their families live.

Like the other families I had visited, the extended family by then collectively owned many more consumable items. Each grown child had access to or owned a television. They each had CD players and radios, and everyone, as in María's family, finally had their own bed; no one sleeps on a petate on the ground any longer. Furthermore, as in both María and Aída's families, they had modern conveniences for personal hygiene. The fact that the families no longer had to use what land they might have behind their house as a toilet, or a bucket of warm water in the house for a bath, means that they treat their physical person quite differently, and, I believe, have come to appreciate their bodies within a different sensibility: with more respect, less deference to others, with a feeling that is decidedly more "modern," and imbued with feelings that the self is entitled to respect and privacy. This change in thinking with reference to their bodily *hexis* is very clear.

CONCLUSION: PLACE AND IDENTITY, LAND AND COMMUNITY

In this chapter I have reviewed the movement of migrants to Oaxaca as they arrived in the 1960s to find a place, a location in which to establish house sites and build their homes and their lives at the edge of urban Oaxaca. At first—with no material resources, no social networks to speak of, and no community to call upon—they used whatever was at hand to build shelter, to make a home, and to establish the first version of this new place. They began with the cheapest materials available that might keep out the elements. In those first years, most of the houses were wattle and daub structures with tarpaper roofs or, in the most up-scale versions, cement rooms, though these were much less common. Most houses had a cook shack next to them where women continued to use a comal as well as a two-burner kerosene stove—both remnants of the rural life of the past. Nowadays, except for the newest houses that are being built far up on the hillside, most houses are made of brick and have tile roofs, and second stories are commonplace. Houses are usually built within compounds, thus creating multiple family dwellings. Perimeter fences routinely surround these compounds, making the streets less open and inviting than before. In place of the older openness, the new structures afford the inhabitants more privacy and security. Their previously fragile attachment to the land, and the similarly delicate forms of family and self-identity that characterized the inhabitants and their homes in the past, have been reinvented. New, more substantial homes, coupled with more clearly urban dispositions, closer attachments to the city, and better-developed connections to the wider global processes of modernization—all are also evident now.

In order make this transition, to secure the necessary and basic services that the community depended upon, as well as to establish land titles, early residents bonded together in the Mesa Directiva and worked together in the tequio. Communal work functioned to give the colonia an identity as a progressive community where "things got done," and enabled them to become organized to lobby the city to include Colonia Hermosa within its boundaries.

Colonia land was fundamental to the relationship that developed between the community and the larger Oaxacan society, and this relationship was structured at various levels on the basis of a complex network of political relations. In the early period of this partnership, the colonos were universally grateful for government help. They always

expressed their humble status in the way they used their bodies: hats
off, heads down—reminding one of obedient school children—when
they were in the presence of public officials and civic leaders. For some,
I would argue that their bodily hexis signals a form of enchantment
in that such misrecognition is inherent in the social relations of state
power and capital, as celebrations focused upon the one-way provision
of gifts from the state, ignoring the self-reliance and hard work of the
colonos. Indeed, during the late 1960s and early 1970s, it appears that
the state had a monopoly over good works through its almost complete control of major economic resources and its domination of local
celebrations. The state (or the PRI) defined celebratory moments in the
colonia by the presence of state officials (the PRI). Such connections
resulted from the mediation of dispositions by objective structures and
habitus. The colonos could not be independent of the city entirely, and,
in fact, as Murphy and Stepick (1991) point out, next to the family, the
state was, by the 1970s, one of the most important social institutions
to community members.

But this early symbiosis changed in the middle of the 1980s, with individual colonia households asking for personal help (not help through
the Mesa Directiva) from competing political parties, and basing their
voting patterns on which party could "deliver" their requests. Communal *requests* were replaced by individual *demands* through the use of
the "political marketplace." This development suggests the emergence
of a citizenry who assume entitlement of favors from the government
and from local party officials.

The process of identity making and community making also involved an argument between residents about land titles, and ultimately
resulted in the original developer spending time in jail for land fraud.
At the time, the different "sides" of the argument were strongly felt, but
by the year 2000, no one discussed this part of their collective history,
and when I brought it up in conversations, it was dismissed as a relic
of the past, no longer important as part of the way residents feel about
themselves today. The early emphasis on community help and migrant
status has shifted to a reliance on property, the ownership of place,
membership in a larger community, and a on the capacities of grown
children. It also depends on a sense of citizenship as members of a city
who are deserving of city services.

The transformation of personal identity and social practice mirrors
the material transformation of the colonia. This transformation began
with an extra-legal settlement, in which place, land, and property were

marginal, illegal, and unsettled, and moved to the present setting: a city suburb, where land titles have been distributed, incomes have been secured, and attachment to place has been established. The struggles of the past—first to find and occupy land, then to legalize and formalize the same land—all this has been put to one side. Just as jobs are valued as much for their longevity as for their income, so too land, and the formalization of the relationship of individuals and families to that land, has been central to a shift in subjectivities. The social habitus within the field of colonia practices has altered in the long struggle to secure symbolic, political, and economic capital. Inhabitants have worked hard, used their resources as best they can, traded in on assets secured through friends, reputation, and family, and have made a place and an identity for themselves in their new location. Thirty years on, their successes stand on the hillside in the form of established houses, secure futures, and less hardship. As they say, they sweated for this success, and this sweat is embedded in the bricks and mortar of these new buildings. The urban poor have moved from an environment of desperation to a life in which at least their basic needs are met. The brilliance of this achievement cannot be overstated. Without resources of any kind except their labor (in most cases) and their strategic use of government help, the community of Colonia Hermosa made itself into an established element of the city. The residents now pay taxes, and they exist in the formal documents of the state. They are no longer marginal—neither in the material conditions of life, nor in their sense of themselves as full citizens.

CHAPTER 5

WORK, MONEY, AND DREAMS:
TRANSFORMING CAPITAL

INTRODUCTION: FIELDS, PRACTICE, AND CAPITALS

THIS CHAPTER EXPLORES THE WORLD of work and money, as well as the mechanism by which such structures influence the lives and identities of Colonia Hermosa residents. In the story that begins the chapter, Alejandro discusses his work history, how that history has unfolded, and how particular events have led him to his present situation. Alejandro's words give weight to the central theoretical argument of this book: that our lives are not simply a matter of chance, though chance has its place. Rather, we can claim that our lives are a product of our personal and family habitus, class habitus, and the structuring structures of economics, politics, and education within which we live. The social space of everyday practice can be likened to a series of social fields (Mahar 1990). In these fields there are positions of strength and weakness—as in a soccer game. In this game, players who have a feel for the game make better choices by virtue of their better placement and because of their *doxic* understanding of what choices mean in the game. In short, their strategies and their struggles for social and symbolic capital are more effective, better established in evidence and experience, and more likely to succeed than the alternatives. Such placements in the field are constituted in two central ways. First, they emerge from structural conditions, such as one's social class, and the possibilities, which are closed or opened up to some, but not to others. Second, we must examine the durable dispositions of individuals, one's "habitus," which is constructed through the learning that goes on with family, friends, schooling, and the like.

In the story that Alejandro relates, we glimpse how both structure and agency play out in his life. There is an additional, third critical aspect of social practice that is appropriate to Alejandro's life. It is this: *social positions in a field and one's habitus are not automatically reproduced.* In other words, lives are not automatically reproduced from the personal history and social class that we come from. As the stories of the family are revealed, readers should mark the differences between the life of Alejandro and that of his older brother Santiago, which are quite distinct in certain important respects: jobs, income, and the prospects for their children's futures. What this means is that even someone with a "weak" position in the field, such as Santiago, can be strategic and struggle in a positive fashion to learn the rules of the game, and thereby change his class position in a positive way.

ALEJANDRO

"I decided to go to work after two and one-half years of secondary school because my mother was so poor.[1] Anyway, I didn't like being in school, and I wasn't very studious, even though when I studied I did get good grades. But I despaired of our economic situation. My mother was working and it was just too hard. And also, I needed money and some things. My friends were neighbors in the colonia. Most were working at various jobs, like delivering water. At that time, I was working in a mechanic shop as an *ayudante* [helper] before I became a plumber. I guess I was about fourteen years old. I stayed working there [at the shop], for about six months. The person I was working for decided to go to Salina Cruz. My mother said no, so I stayed in Oaxaca. Also at that time I remember that I wanted to learn how to drive—my brother too. More than anything, I wanted to drive.

"There was a Senior Fausto, an *albañil* [a stone mason]. Well, he arrived on the scene one day and said, 'What are you doing, *chamaco* [young boy]?' I was just in front of our house. 'Well,' he says, 'this guy, who later became my compadre, needs some help with some plumbing work.' 'OK,' I said, 'Sure. I want to work. When do we start?' 'Tomorrow. We'll see.' 'Seriously?' 'Yes, I'll be waiting for you at my house.' So the next day I went along to the next colonia, and his neighbor was the plumber, and he said to the guy, 'Look, here's the chamaco that I was telling you about—he wants a job.' And so I began working for him. We were working in the city, and then they went to work in Vera Cruz. So, they said to me, 'Let's go to the coast, to the port to work.' 'Yes, but it's so far, it'll take so long to get there . . .' So, I went anyway, and we stayed about fifteen days, perhaps a month. Basically we went between

Oaxaca and the coast working for about four years. We worked on the penitentiary. It was contract work for the federal government. They paid by the hour. That was when the boss taught me to drive. Then, I taught my brother. He didn't want to at first, but now he's a driver for Superagua (the local water bottling plant).

"Truly, I never repented not finishing, or going to school. I got more satisfaction by helping my mother. When I could help her that's what I really liked. And she would always help me. At this time she was sewing traditional clothing for a man who sold things in the central market. He also brought clothes to the United States to sell. He paid her, more or less, pretty well. So we put our money together. I always gave her the money, less the money I needed for my expenses.

"I first worked with Ishmael, the master plumber, and then I left and worked for about thirteen years on a job with a construction crew. When you came in 1996, I was not working. At this time the government was changing too. Under Salinas de Gortari our money ran out, and then there was devaluation, and with this change all our work disappeared. There was so much unemployment. People were paid very little and could not earn their living. I would go out and help friends as a driver, to carry stuff, so I was working as a helper for them—they were not compadres, just acquaintances, just friends.

"What my wife doesn't understand is that we have suffered in order to have come up so much, to have come to where we are now. I think we have come up because we lived a good life, no matter where we were, or in which condition—even when my mother's house collapsed. We had a very low economic position. If my father had been with us, well, it would have been very different. But right now, we have achieved something."

COLONIA HERMOSA, 1968–1975

Walking up the wide, ascending dirt path that served as a "main street" in Colonia Hermosa in those early days, one first passed the primary school on the left, and Guzmán's mother's house and baths on the right. Further up, adobe and cement houses, each painted different pastel colors, sat side by side until this pattern of building in close proximity was made impossible by the steep hillside. In each house, the front door was open, whether it be the dry or rainy season, and the predominantly floral print window curtains would be tied into a knot so that the light could enter. The radio or, in the 1970s, the television would be playing.

In a few of these houses, a small *tienda,* or shop, was established in the main room, which also served as a bedroom at night. During the day, it was mostly women and children who populated the street and the ascending paths, visiting back and forth between houses, the school, the shops, and the communal water faucets.

The household was the hub of daily activity in Colonia Hermosa. In the late 1960s and 1970s it was the nexus for the production and accumulation of capital, economic as well as cultural. Colonia families inevitably structured their households and their daily practice on the basis of the limits that they faced. Households and families were limited by the general constraints of material poverty, and the immediate need for basic necessities: food, shelter, and medical care. There were also general community requirements of water, lights, sewer lines, and the need for government recognition in order to obtain land titles. It was toward these goals—personal, familial, and communal—that people worked each day.

During the period 1968 to 1975, the accumulation of economic capital started to take place among those who were, by the social standards of the colonia, "successful." The general consensus was that certain families had started by accumulating cultural capital, which had been formed in three areas: schooling and occupational training for children, higher-status marriage partners for children, and the acquisition of high-status material items such as clothing, household goods, and certain types of food. Such cultural capital was then transformable back into economic capital, as better social relationships in the community and beyond, as well as job training, which brought back better jobs and income to the community. In this way, capitals circulated, and, as well, there was a transformation in the kinds of capitals available, and in the amount of capital that was available to the community as a whole.

By 1999–2000 a similar history was familiar to all of my key Colonia Hermosa informants. What I had not expected, however, were the differences in the rates of success (as they measured success) between siblings. In some families the difference was very marked, providing interesting example of the process of class transformation through their use of personal agency and their choices of strategies. These differences are clearly evident in the variety of occupations, housing, and incomes that now characterize the larger extended families. For instance, consider the differences between Alejandro and his elder brother Santiago, or the life of Consuelo as compared to the lives of her sisters. In these lives, changes in personal habitus and strategy are revealed in spite of family members having come to adulthood within the same family. Thus, while the larger structures of class remain, individuals can and do change class positions.

SOCIAL GROUPINGS AND WORK

Residents of Colonia Hermosa had early on categorized themselves into three broad social groups based on types of employment and the presumed benefits and wages that they might earn. "The wealthy" were defined as people who were living in some ease with regard to money and goods, and whose houses were made of cement and brick— in other words, more substantial than wattle and daub or adobe brick. They were not short of food day-to-day. Then, there were "the regulars," characterized by having a steady income and thus not having to continually borrow food or money from neighbors or compadres. Finally there were "the poor," or the unskilled laborers, living hand-to-mouth each day. These locally defined categories were in consonance with the more generalized sociological groupings from our research completed in the early 1970s.[2]

At that time, Colonia Hermosa residents categorized the occupational structure of the colonia into four groups: professional, skilled labor, home entrepreneur, and unskilled labor. Among the 192 workers from 100 households, these were the categories of work that were found:

Professional: A category that included those whose educational level
was beyond secondary school. The 35 persons from this sample
were teachers, secretaries, military personnel, businessmen, and
accountants. Their monthly wage level ranged from $190 to $450.
The average wage was $287 per month in 1972.[3]

Skilled Labor: Of the 62 persons in this group, the average level of
education was five years of primary school. Jobs in this category
included bus and truck drivers, mechanics, painters, carpenters,
seamstresses, factory workers, and tailors. Monthly salaries ranged
from $10 to $128. The average monthly wage was $69 per month in
1972.

Home Entrepreneurs: Of the 56 people in this category, the average
level of education was two years of primary school. Jobs ranged

from food vendors, laundresses, tortilla makers, small tienda owners (in their private homes), piecework seamstresses, and baby-sitters. The monthly wage range was $3 to $64. The average monthly wage was $34.

Unskilled Labor: Of the 39 people in this category, the average level of education was the same as that of the home entrepreneurs: two years of primary schooling. Their jobs ranged from day laborers, do-mestic workers, and stevedores to bathhouse and gas station atten-dants. They worked outside the house, unlike the home entrepre-neurs, but in casual employment. Wages earned ranged from $7 to $50 a month. The average wage was $29 per month.

The city of Oaxaca and the surrounding valley have developed since the 1970s into a modern metropolitan center accessed by a new high-way, trains, and buses. It has become a large, sprawling metropolitan region anchored by the city of Oaxaca. Because of the general economic crisis in Mexico during the late 1970s and 1980s, the mean household income for the city fell by more than half.[4] For those who had jobs that complied with the minimum wage requirements and that carried some benefits, income was reduced by 56 percent. Those workers who were largely unskilled suffered a 51 percent reduction. These statistics mean that each worker could support fewer dependents, and thus the situation increased the need for strategic borrowing and job network-ing, both of which necessitated the use of social capital in its many forms. Those who were well connected fared better than those who were isolated. As well, in many families, children such as Alejandro and Consuelo needed to work instead of going to school. Necessity drives a hard bargain. By the late 1990s, with the further devaluation of the peso, the necessity for older children to combine their incomes and living sites with those of their aging parents and siblings was still an important strategic choice. But in making a virtue of necessity, as Bourdieu would say, it allowed families to subsist, to survive, and later, even to prosper. This was a new form of social strategizing that helped families to prosper, but informants were not aware of the possibili-ties at the time. What is interesting is that even now, no one (without prompting) mentions living together as a strategy to better the family. It may be that this is simply taken for granted, a practice accepted and used without thinking. As such, it is a different sort of strategic sensi-bility than getting a job or an education.

In Colonia Hermosa, residents' connection to Oaxacan and Mexican society occurred largely through the residents' aspirations to the same mainstream, bourgeois norms and goals that were already embedded in the country's orthodox social structure. In the late 1960s and early 1970s such aspirations were easy to list: jobs, educational opportunities for children, medical facilities, and a general desire to be more closely in touch with the world. By the mid-1970s some families were considered successful within the colonia because they had moved from the subproletarian "hand-to-mouth" world of survival to the Mexican working class, with steady pay and some benefits. As one informant said: "Well, yes, there are some who are of, as we say, the middle class or rich, right here in the colonia. Why do we say that? Well, because they have a good job with a monthly salary that they can count on. And their children, well, they all go to school for job training." Each resident sought to be part of mainstream society, but they were often prevented from getting there by Mexico's system of class stratification, the poor management of the Mexican economy, too little money of their own, and their own dispositions (Mahar 2000), which were not suited to playing the "game" of the developing urban economy.

SAVING AND CREATING CAPITAL

In the 1960s and 1970s, individuals and their families used whatever strategies were at hand to survive, whenever and however they could be managed, through jobs, social networks, and by trading household goods. As previously mentioned, the jobs through which people were able to earn cash ranged from service occupations, such as errand boys, to construction laborers, helpers on second-class buses, food vendors, and women who worked in their homes doing laundry, making tortillas, and sewing on contract for market vendors. These were the basic sources of their limited economic capital. Social capital was derived from the social networks established through the Mesa Directiva, family, compadres, and neighborhood friends. Social networks were used repeatedly to supply food, money, child care, and other basic amenities. Thus social capital could be transformed into economic capital in particular contexts. As well, household goods, such as treadle sewing machines and radios, were used repeatedly as items to pawn for money. In some sense, pawned items were a type of savings account for people who did not use banks. They were usually redeemed and then used in the pawnshop again. This, for colonia residents, was a strategy that they often discussed. Thus the value of an item was not only its use value, but the value at the pawn shop when owners needed extra cash. Of course, this also meant that not everything was redeemed.

Given the occupational list and the incomes that went along with such occupations, it is clear that most residents of Colonia Hermosa worked each day solely for that day's living. Such things as banks, savings accounts, and credit cards were not used. Concepts such as abstract economic calculation, saving money for the future, and the concept of a surplus of money were absent for most families in the early years of colonia development. There are several reasons that can help to account for these behavioral and conceptual problems: first and foremost, poverty and the small amounts of money that residents had at their disposal; second, problems of illiteracy; third, lack of experience with financial institutions; and finally, the manifestly unwelcoming environment, for the poor, of institutional offices of banks and financial entities.

This is not to say, however, that other forms of credit did not exist. In the early years of Colonia Hermosa's development, complex credit systems in the colonia itself existed and were widely used. Credit was extended to locals by colonia stores, appliances and jewelry were pawned, neighbors and compadres and kin shared food, child care was shared, and sometimes money was loaned between families and individuals. There were, in fact, elaborate, though informal credit and borrowing structures. At one time these arrangements generally took the form of reciprocal exchanges. Sometimes, especially from wealthier compadres or family, loans were given to meet a crisis situation, such as a trip to the hospital. These loans were often not paid back as money, but through help in the form of labor. A sort of labor credit also could be established. This is the kind of informal reciprocal gift exchange that exists among many traditional and small populations. Also, some colonia families would loan money to local residents at high rates of interest, 15 percent compounded weekly, or sometimes daily.[5] In fact, this sort of borrowing continued into the year 2000, making some residents of Colonia Hermosa very wealthy. Their colonia properties now mimic those in the city, with large fences and gates around them, a second story, bars on the first-story windows, and nicely managed gardens. These residents also have expensive cars, as opposed to the older Volkswagens, taxis, or broken-down American cars that are commonplace in Colonia Hermosa and throughout other hillside neighborhoods.

My informants' discussions of daily expenses and income during the

1968–1974 period always focused on the present. Listening to the way they managed their lives, it often seemed that their payment for daily colonia expenses was more of a "stealing from Peter to pay Paul" exercise, or a balancing act where all household resources were used at one time or another to survive an immediate crisis. Families did not list their projected incomes and possible outgoings for the week. Instead, they lived and bought goods on a daily basis because a balanced allocation of daily and weekly expenses was not possible. Daily survival is not the sort of activity that can be easily planned on a balance sheet. Furthermore, most colonia families did not have the capital or the dispositions to do so. However, there were exceptions to the rule, and thus there were substantial changes. By 1999, some of my informants and most of their children were experienced with financial institutions, as well as with government-sponsored credit offices. One family that began to bake whole-wheat bread in the colonia as a small business to supplement the husband's income as a shop clerk now has two bread shops in town, as well as their bakery and shop in Colonia Hermosa. One of their daughters has become an accountant and has organized their financial affairs, and their sons work for the company. As their business grew and their ability to purchase more land grew, the children built their homes in one of the two family compounds. One compound remains in Colonia Hermosa, and the other is in a neighboring colonia. Their common work became a huge entrepreneurial success.

DAILY SURVIVAL AND STRATEGIES FOR THE FUTURE

Family budgets and business budgets (for doing laundry, making tamales to sell, and so on) were usually confused together in that profit and expenses were mixed. As most families were unfamiliar with common business practices, formal calculability in a small, home-based store that runs on a large number of small transactions was therefore almost entirely lacking. The lack of calculability did have one advantage, however: people did not compute the poor exchange between the low income from their work as opposed to their labor and production costs. What their daily reckonings reveal are a variety of economic dispositions and ways of managing.

In the early days of Colonia Hermosa, residents often talked about having a three-part plan to manage their daily expenses. One category was general expenses, which included household costs such as utility bills, medical expenses, installment payments (usually for household goods), and clothing costs. Then, second, there were household payments, which included food and transportation allowances and payment of small debts to local food stores. Finally, there were business expenses, which included all home entrepreneurial costs.[6]

Those who were defined as "wealthy" by colonia residents in 1971 had a monthly income of about 1,500 old Mexican pesos ($165 US). Families such as these spent far more money than average families on food and budgeted for time payments and utilities.[7] Families invested in their children's education, proceeded to support them through primary and secondary training, and helped toward some professional training. This is much like Aída's approach, ensuring that her eldest son, Santiago, could complete his schooling. This was the future.

Others held to different dispositions, even though they said that they hoped that their children would be educated. Some focused on everyday expenses and put nothing aside. Some would not keep their children in school if they were needed at home. Others depended upon a kind of spiritualized rationality. They refused a middle-class type of future orientation, believing that long-term outcomes were in the hands of God, the Virgin, and a variety of Catholic saints. So, for instance, instead of ensuring that her oldest children stayed in school, María preferred to undertake a pilgrimage to the coast, to the shrine of the Virgin of Juquila, in order to secure the well-being of her family. For her, life experiences were a result of fate, God's will, or the will of their favorite saint. This is a completely comprehensible view, because coming from extreme poverty, such a class habitus is intricately tied to families and individuals who never have any resources with which to plan. Economic planning was therefore meaningless. Successful strategies for them were, in part, within the structure of patron and client string pulling and the use of strategic networks between neighbors, but other strategies existed powerfully for them in the world of mystical reasoning.

During these early years, one can visualize Colonia Hermosa as its own economic universe where people like Aída, Margarita, María, Leticia, and Isabel and her family could survive in their various ways. The colonia provided an environment in which earners with very low incomes could maintain equilibrium between basic necessities and expenditures, especially in building and owning their own homes. It was an equilibrium that allowed for better housing because residents could better manage overall expenses if they did not have to pay rent or a mortgage. The emerging status of ownership of these humble properties provided families with the much-needed security to move forward economically, and to survive more easily because they had permanent shelter. Other expenses, such as time payments on cooking pots or furniture, or the cost of electricity (which in the early 1970s most families did not have), were very small and flexible as to payment dates. The drawbacks of time payments were (and are) that interest accrued on those debts. Consequently, colonia residents sometimes paid double the initial cost for an item without recognizing that they had done so. Isabel, for example, bought her double bed on time payments and ended up paying for it three times over. Such arrangements are never helpful to the poor and, in fact, are punishing to those most in need.

ECONOMIC AND CULTURAL CAPITAL:
SOCIAL RANK IN COLONIA HERMOSA

In a series of interviews, twenty-two families representative of Colonia Hermosa were asked to rank other particular families. The point of this exercise was to understand how the residents constructed their social world and its divisions. Such views do change over time, so it is important to note that the particular snapshot that follows was taken in the years 1969–1970 by Michael Higgins.[8] The attributes that these residents employed are very similar to the village patterns observed by Lynn Stephen (1991: 30). There were three distinct dimensions of stratification: wealth, occupation, and respect. As well, we found that particular subjective dispositions were attached to each dimension, and that each occurred in particular fields or social contexts. The meaning of each dimension was more subtle and complex than the words "wealth," "occupation," and "respect" imply. As a result, I would further describe the dimensions used by the colonos along the lines of Bourdieu (1990b): as economic, cultural, and symbolic capital.

As previously mentioned, colonia residents defined themselves and others as being "poor" (living hand-to-mouth each day); just "regular," which was defined as not having to continually borrow food or money from neighbors or compadres; or "wealthy," defined primarily by informants' perceptions of ease with regard to available money and goods. However, such categorization by others was not always consistent; more complex factors entered into such identifications. Given that several dimensions of hierarchy are involved, this is not surprising.

The amount of personal goods in a household carried with it both symbolic and economic expressions, as these consumables were not defined just in relation to steady work but to a *steady life*. Such goods, it was argued, derived from a broadly serious approach to all things and were thus a clear indication of a holder of high symbolic capital. As well, these items were often pawned and, as mentioned earlier, acted as a kind of savings account and source of ready cash.

SYMBOLIC CAPITAL

In the early days of the Colonia Hermosa settlement, residents defined social status or symbolic capital as being embedded in one's reputation and personal networks with friends or compadres, who themselves had to be of "good standing," and who were thus equally serious and hard working, and dedicated to their families. Since economic capital was hard to find in the early years, symbolic capital was a treasured asset. And it was not merely pleasant to be afforded high social status. Such standing had direct material consequences: in the amount of money that could be borrowed, the food that would be shared, and the amount of debt that could be run up at the grocery store. Such qualities made survival a little easier than it otherwise might have been. During this period of development, colonia residents categorized one another with regard to their willingness to help with community and tequio work groups—in short, on the basis of their symbolic capital. Not all residents wanted to be part of a group, even though they might benefit in the long term. Aída, whose life was discussed in Chapter 4, was respected in the colonia because she devoted herself to raising her children, did not have boyfriends, and always contributed work with the tequio groups. In 1969, she said of the tequio: "Yes, I do help now and then, and I always help to cook for the fiestas when officials come. Although there are a few women, part of the Mesa Directiva, who try to be bosses, they seem to take home food too."

María, whose family was not respected because of her husband's weekend binges, and because of her own graphic language, refused to help with the tequio. She responded to the question of her participation by saying:

No. No, why should I? If I need something at home, my husband will see to it or a compadre will help us. What do I want to get involved with Guzmán and his group for? They are people who just think of themselves. Of course it's good that the colonia has some water faucets and some lights, but I don't get involved with those people. How can I anyway, with so much work to do, and so many children to look after? I have plenty to do here with the washing, cooking and my children.

Most generally, symbolic capital has been defined as a sense of honor, reputation, dignity, prestige, or power. Symbolic capital is the most critical form of capital, as both precapitalist and capitalist societies are organized around it. Indeed, symbolism, meaning, and the apparently nonmaterial are profoundly important in structuring our lives. For example, divisions and subdivisions based on tastes, aesthetic judgment, social hierarchy, and methods of discernment act in powerful ways as mechanisms of social classification. This is apparent in the establishment of any hierarchy, and in the maintenance and struggle over the most material of systems: class structures. Thus, particular behaviors, ways of speaking, forms of dressing, and types of community activity all work as class or position markers—even in a squatter settlement as economically homogeneous as Colonia Hermosa. By 2000, the import of symbolic capital within the colonia as part of its local ranking system had lessened, as ties between colonos themselves became less important, and community-wide ties weakened. Today, although residents might discuss the wealth of their neighbors, it is from a distance. No longer do neighbors discuss behavior patterns that they do not approve of, unless it is within their own extended families. Now that Colonia Hermosa is a recognized suburb, the focal point of economic and cultural behaviors is the city of Oaxaca and beyond, as adult children work outside of the colonia and, sometimes, outside of the city and across the border in the United States.

In the early years of my work in Colonia Hermosa, symbolic capital (status, honor, and prestige) was of the utmost importance in creating and maintaining the social capital that is bound to one's social relationships. Living a life worthy of respect was what counted most. At one time, members of the Mesa Directiva were considered to have a significant measure of symbolic capital based on their work for the colonia. In fact, those who had no such reputation tried to buy prestige through thinly veiled "good deeds." Symbolic capital mattered on its own account. The importance of symbolic capital in the field of social relations was more determinant than other forms of capital when it came to social relationships between households. As of the year 2000, symbolic capital within a family, and especially between siblings, was still regarded as a powerful measure of respect, but much less so among neighboring households. In the early years of colonia development, economic, social, and cultural capital were important, but in order to have a position in the field of social relations, and in order to be a patron, one must have converted such forms of capital into symbolic capital. In time this changed.

CULTURAL CAPITAL

A second type of capital that is important to social life in Colonia Hermosa is cultural capital. This, itself symbolic, refers to skills and knowledge, one's educational and professional qualifications, and the like. This quality continues to be a topic of conversation in the colonia, as it was thirty years ago, with regard to material wealth and to educational and job success. So, for instance, residents who knew Aída before she left the colonia still regard her highly and often praise her oldest son for his ability to overcome their dire poverty, complete his schooling, and meet his career goals. Others will praise the new style of neighbors: the remodeled house, the car, and the clothes. Previously in the colonia such display of cultural wealth did not exist, even though there were economic differences, as is clear from different levels of occupations discussed above. Neighbors usually limited their comments to whether or not husbands were treating their wives well, whether a family was struggling for daily survival, or how active a family was in colonia activities.

Thus education, a mechanism directly of value for occupational and economic advancement, came to the fore most directly after the first stages of settlement, at a time when such opportunities started to appear. However, the critical point about the forms of capital is not so much the definition of the different types of capital, but the relationship between capital as a symbolic structure, and capital defined as part of the social structure. While one would not argue that symbolic structures create social structure, I argue that the symbolic is much more than an instrument of knowledge. These social forms are to be understood as principles of vision and division, which allow individuals not only to create a reality, but also to believe in that reality. Within certain limits, therefore, symbolic structures have an extraordinary and underestimated power of constitution.[9] Given that cultural capital in the form of education, social goods, and so forth came into prominence in the 1970s and 1980s, it provided a genuine source of power for those who recognized and used it.

LABOR, CAPITAL, AND STRATEGY

Today, as they were in the late 1960s, workers from Colonia Hermosa are often employed in service-oriented occupations—a situation that reflects the phenomenon of underemployment rather than unemployment. For instance, doing laundry, making food to sell, sewing on contract to a market stallholder, or selling popsicles on the street are jobs that do not require the full-time engagement of those employed. Being in this sector means that colonia residents have a marginal income in terms of the larger society, but these occupations are not marginal to the social structure of the city since Oaxaca depends on their work. Sadly, such employment does not allow workers a steady income, and in their situation, the importance of steady employment and income cannot be overemphasized. It is the steadiness of work that, again, is of greatest of value. And this value lies in the quality of calculability that this form of employment affords. All of the colonia residents who became economically successful in the city were able to do so because they secured steady jobs and enough money for basic necessities. Certain types of service work, such as being a waitress in a tourist restaurant (as was Adelina before she gave birth to her daughter), provide a steady income and perhaps benefits, but other service work, such as painting the small wooden animal carvings (the work of Consuelo's brother Moises) may offer only a marginal income and no health benefits.

For some, success based upon a steady job occurred within the parental generation (for example, in the lives of Isabel and Arturo), whereas others built family success around their children's jobs and education. Mastery of the future was dependent upon the degree of calculability implicit in certain work relations, upon the objective conditions of income, health care, and educational possibilities, which collectively ensured at least the possibility of success. Unless this shift in occupational location occurred, the only possible attitude of colonia residents to their lives was a kind of traditionalism. It was not a copy of village tradition, because that life does not exist in the city. Rather, it constituted the sort of revisionist traditional ideology that has within it the possibility of different strategies and practices, given the correct conditions, while at the same time containing within it the impossibility of enacting any such strategy. The tendency for families like that of María and Alfredo to see life experiences as a result of fate, God's will, or the will of their favorite saint is due, in part, to their inability to plan a future within the confines of developing capitalism and globalization.

Life for them was a matter of chance, not amenable to planning based on economic calculation.

The lack of Western strategies with regard to economic behavior was obvious among some colonia families, in a material sense, in their management of money and in the types of household goods that constituted the elements of cultural capital. The strategies of reproduction and conversion of cultural capital indicated a preference for Western over traditional goods, for modern cookware over earthen ware, and an attempt to accumulate certain types of appliances, such as blenders, radios, and, for some by 1974, a television. Western tastes in all cases trumped traditional tastes, even when Western goods were not functional or useful. Their money was organized around a preference for cash in hand, and dominant attitudes favored manageable time payments to salesmen who came door-to-door around the colonia. As mentioned, Isabel and Arturo bought a double bed and ended up paying for it three times over because of the interest on time payments.

A second example of poor economic strategy resulting from a family's poverty centers on the question of pig-raising. Residents would often say they had made a profit from raising a pig, when in actuality more money had been spent buying and raising the animal than had been earned through its sale. Or, consider the experiences of María, who often sold enchiladas on the streets of Oaxaca. One time, for instance, she spent approximately 150 pesos to prepare the food, but earned on the street only 100 to 175 pesos. When asked, she said that she had earned 175 pesos, because that was the amount of cash she had from the sale. The cost of supplies and labor was not included. But this kind of analysis is somewhat beside the point. What I noticed thirty years ago, and what has stayed with me, is the impression that as part of a women's work, making food for sale ensured that her family would have leftovers and that they would be "special"—that is, it meant that the family would have not just beans and tortillas, but tamales or enchiladas. And there was much more going on than economic calculation. If all that mattered was money, then this would have been a bemusing strategy. But instead it produced family food and gave people an excuse for a festive meal, thus enriching their social life and marking off the market days from the ordinary. Having an excuse to go off to town was welcome for women at home; again, it made the day special, filled the project with meaning and purpose, and reflected the effort of the women involved to be creative beyond the household. Consequently, I came to conclude that the apparently economic activity was, in fact, social and cultural at its base, as are many other activities. These processes are much more akin to the accumulation of social capital, of being able to afford a holiday or a fiesta, than they are a mere exercise in economic calculation.

The dispositions of the families I studied thus reflect their abilities to enact a series of creative reinventions to transform symbolic, economic, and cultural capital. Aída held to the "saintly" model of motherhood, a typical characterization of traditional life, even as she prepared her son for the city. Alfredo worked at the edges of the market economy, while his wife appealed to the Catholic saints for their long-term needs. Isabel and Arturo, with their Zapotec and Mazatec origins, both saw the world in a traditional Indian manner, and were seen by city residents as inhabitants of that other world. Yet they both worked as street traders, making a living on the edge of an alien world. Each family had thus constructed a unique solution to a set of complex economic problems. These forms of economic and social practices constituted their adaptations to the city. Every scrap of clothing, every penny earned was necessary for day-to-day living in the colonia. The household was the site of these struggles. Nowadays, as colonos are most deeply anchored within the fields of economic production in a developing capitalist economy, it is economic capital and individual achievement, conceived of as symbolic capital, that is critical to the residents' drive for success and a hopeful future.

POLITICAL PRACTICE AS STRATEGY

By 2000, the original field of social practice in Colonial Hermosa no longer existed. Those who once held the dominant social and political positions in the community were no longer interested in accumulating the cultural and symbolic capital that this once offered them; their positions vis-à-vis the city had become more important. They had moved from the subproletariat to the working class. The social practices that they had previously valued, and by which they had secured their first footholds in Oaxaca, were no longer important. Now they are connected to the upward movement of their employment trajectories as they move from one class to another. The original fields of social and political practice have been replaced by the domain of the market, and many of the previous cargo (office) holders have become small shopkeepers and owners. They are no longer interested in reproducing their positions within the colonia, but instead are intent on reproducing and advancing their own positions more broadly in the city and, by extension, the positions of their children within the wider marketplace. This is all in keeping with sensible urban practices and strategies. The colonia residents' original strategies of creative reinvention of capitals have been dissolved by the social logic of the city. The field of politics, and of gaining political power and capital, has altered dramatically as the field of the colonia opened up through the broader connections to the city that incorporation as a suburb required.

An interesting aspect of political life during the first two decades of colonia development is that residents did not openly recognize that the power generated from a leader's political capital also enhanced his or her economic life and gave them a lift in social class within the colonia. The behavior of the Guzmán family was, in those early days, understood as honorable in a *disinterested* fashion, in the way that traditional village leadership is defined, so that all calculation was hidden under the shroud of honor and disinterest. Sr. Guzmán's self-interest, and that of others on the Mesa Directiva, was misrecognized by residents, hidden by a mask of symbolic capital. I am not suggesting that the residents were in any way duped, but it seems to me that the reason for this lack of recognition, as reflected in the daily conversations that I had with them, is clear: there was a struggle between residents and the city over the rights of settlers to the land they had taken for house sites. Thus the leaders of Colonia Hermosa's political action were seen as working on behalf of the community as a whole, and not solely for their personal gain. Of course, both interpretations are accurate. As the colonia developed basic necessities, and as certain individuals developed the first market, such leadership was understood more cynically as being self-serving. By the late 1970s, economic rather than traditional symbolic capital had become the deciding factor in the struggle over political positions, a shift that brought about corresponding changes in the fields of social practice and political activity. Because the very nature of capital had changed, the criteria defining success had become largely economic. But the community as a whole had also prospered from the actions of self-interested individuals. The fact that unsuccessful individuals no longer gained symbolic capital from their colonia positions was irrelevant.

Today, symbolic capital seems to lie closer to home. It resides within the family and is linked to the responsibility that family members take for one another, as well for living a decent, moral life. For instance, symbolic capital can be seen at work in the way individuals are generous to each other when they can be, and whether or not they work hard, even if they are not economically successful. In this way the social practices of hard work and responsibility in terms of family and financial obligations can be converted into symbolic capital; these mirror the earlier forms of symbolic capital in the colonia. Thus the shape of the social field and the kinds of capitals struggled over have altered significantly. This change corresponds directly to the transformation of colonos over the past thirty years from migrants to urban citizens. The capital for which most colonos actively struggle is economic capital, which reflects the interests of those residents who conceive of a Western future. Only privately, within the family, does the importance of symbolic capital survive. This is connected to familial help to deserving relatives. Within the larger community, symbolic capital is important to create a good impression, but as neighbors lack the intimacy they once had, the role that such capital has between neighbors has changed.

CONCLUSION

Life in Colonia Hermosa has always been busy with the practical work of making ends meet. It has always been full of work. Nevertheless, despite the poverty that many residents faced—and even when many residents, such as Alejandro and Consuelo, experienced long periods of desolation and despair because of their poverty—the colonia was never dismal. In part, the residents' sustained willingness to give their life to work, and to what they define as success, can be attributed to the optimism of youth; the generation that first settled in Colonia Hermosa was young, most families had very young children, and very few had grown up within the permanent structures of urban poverty that so hamper the lives of the poor, who, as Oscar Lewis described, hand poverty down from generation to generation. A second dimension of the problem is the collective nature of early colonia work. However, in spite of their own best efforts, residents paid heavily for government mismanagement of the national economy. During the period between my early and late fieldwork sessions, an analysis by Murphy and Stepick (1991), which consisted of two random surveys of 1,500 households in 1977 and 600 households in 1987, found that within that decade the percentage of households with no access to job-related fringe benefits had risen from 40 to 60 percent. Henry Selby (1991: xiii) wrote that his interviews with working-class people from 1987 and 1990 indicate that for them the financial crisis was a permanent fact of life. The stories of Alejandro, Adelina, and Moises are testimony that colonia residents truly suffered.

Facts and figures, however, do not give the complete picture. During this same period, the government simultaneously provided some much needed assistance to those needing jobs and housing. During the 1980s, the federal government intensified its economic role by increasing employment in the public sector and in construction from 9.7 percent of all workers in 1970 to 21.9 percent in 1977. In many of the stories that my informants have told about their jobs and income, the federal government has played an important role in their ability to be part of what some call the "aspiring" class, which sits between the minimum-wage and middle-elite income groups.[10] Consider, for example, Consuelo's father, who benefited from new federal construction projects in and around Oaxaca. When I first met Alfredo, he was often only casually employed in construction as a day laborer. At the time, a PRI (government) affiliated union existed, but most construction workers like Alfredo did not belong. He and other non-union laborers would gather between 6 and 7 a.m. at the zócalo, waiting for pickup trucks whose drivers would be looking for ten to fifteen laborers. Social networking was important here, too, as employers would try to hire workers they already knew. In the end, these networks helped Alfredo get a federal construction job, which gave him secure work. With a federal job, Alfredo and his family were not only sure of a wage, but of social security health benefits as well. It is important to understand that in most such cases there is no written agreement, and therefore no legal recourse should verbal agreements dissolve. So, while this meant that for the first time in his life Alfredo had a bimonthly salary and health coverage through the Social Security Hospital, his work was still not based on a legal contract, but on his social connections. As long as the verbal agreement between Alfredo and his contractor worked, his job carried on. But because Alfredo was not a union member, should the agreement have been broken for whatever reason, he would not have had help from to the legal system. The same type of labor agreement characterized Alejandro's work experience as a plumber for the contracting firm that built a federal penitentiary.

The federal government was also important in training and employing many teenagers in Colonia Hermosa by teaching them regional dances at the local technical college, which lies across the highway from the colonia. After completing this course, young people were paid by the government to travel to schools and local villages to dance in fiestas, thereby keeping some of the traditional music and dances alive for Oaxacans. Oaxaca has also had a huge growth in the tourist industry, particularly during the 1980s. Many hotels hire dancers to entertain the tourists, most of whom are from Mexico's middle and elite classes. Dancers also perform at the large Oaxacan fiesta, the Guelaguetza. Work in the tourist sector has not been limited to trained traditional dancers but has opened up to other colonia residents who have become hotel clerks and cleaners, taxi drivers, health care workers, and producers of tourist items to sell.

Finally, since the late 1970s, local educational opportunities have expanded. Many of the children of my original informants have been able to take advantage of the chance to attend school. There has been steady construction and upgrading of technical and professional schools, as well as primary, secondary, and preparatory institutions. Thus individuals such as Consuelo's sister Marisol and Santiago's wife, Alicia, were able to train as nurses in the technical college across the street from the colonia. Flor, Isabel's daughter, also benefited from the extension of state and federal educational programs as she was able to earn her certificate to become a rural schoolteacher. (At the time, the requirement was to complete secondary school, grades 10–12.) If it had not been, in part, for the investment that the government made in the "structure of work" in Oaxaca, these first-generation colonos might have continued to suffer as their parents did through the underemployment, low wages, and lack of benefits associated with unskilled labor. As it stands now, most second-generation colonos do not have to live as urban subproletarians.

As beneficial as many of the changes have been for Colonia Hermosa residents, including increased employment within the federal government in Oaxaca, there has also been a developing division between the formal and informal occupational sectors (Murphy and Stepick 1991). One result is that the distinction between the very poor and those with minimum-wage incomes has become more marked. In the colonia, this is materially evident as the poorest new residents are forced to trek high up the hillside to cut their new house sites out of very steep pieces of ground, and then have to walk long distances down to the bus and into town to sell their wares on the streets, to beg, or to look for contract labor jobs.

Of these new migrants, my informants say that the government should provide industries so that they can work. When Aída sees people selling on the streets or around the markets, or working as day laborers in construction, she comments that if the government does not play a part in job creation, Oaxaca will have more children and beggars on the street. Margarita, who begins our next chapter on social relationships, has the last word here. Her somewhat ambiguous statements about the connection between work, individuals, and government responsibility reflect the views of other informants about what government could do to help the work situation of the Oaxacan populace:

> I think that there are a lot of people without work, but there are also a lot of lazy people—and irresponsible people. But, I feel that if the government created some industries, offering work to these people, I think the people would do it. There are some people already old, who also need work and want to work, or want to continue working, but employers will not take them. They want just the very young. Now, these older people with skills, what do they do? They can't find work. The government seems not to bother about this. Because if they did care, we wouldn't see unemployed people. And how are these people going to go out of their own country, to find work and work very hard to bring their money here? This is a bad thing. A lot of people go away, and send their money back here. I know about lots of people who have cars and houses because they went to the United States. Some don't have papers: the majority don't have papers. They pay a *pollero* [a person who smuggles Mexicans into the United States]. The government ought to educate the young and to teach them skills. Everyone should go to preparatory school and technical school because that teaches them some type of work. (Margarita, 1996)

CHAPTER 6

SOCIAL CAPITAL AS A STRATEGIC CHOICE

SOCIAL RELATIONS FORM THE BASIS of social capital, and they are the focus of this chapter. Social capital shapes a field of strategic play that aids in the survival of households and families. But this does not mean that all social relationships are merely strategic: most people are not consciously calculating or cynical in everyday life. Nevertheless, on the basis of friendship, compadrazgo, and basic good will, Colonia Hermosa residents have come together to create bonds that further community, and by doing so, they have formed social connections that help families with day-to-day expenses and support. In the early years of colonia development, and as recently as the year 2000, such relationships have remained part of the safety net that helps to support residents, although most support these days comes from the extended family.

As part of a system of strategic choices, social relationships are not used in the kind of cold calculation that we imagine is central to corporate life or government activities. However, many personal relationships, such as compadrazgo or even neighborhood support between women, have embedded in them, as always, the expectation of mutual help, either between friends or within the traditional patron-client system of Mexico.

As one reads the stories of Colonia Hermosa residents, it is valuable to remember how, over a period of thirty years, the early, community-wide system of support through social relations and the exchange of social capital has changed qualitatively in both form and substance. Families now are much more insular in that they rely upon and often serve the strength of the natal unit. More important now is residents' social capital as it benefits the family. This is not meant to imply all social capital is ignored outside of the family. Certainly not. In the workplace, the exchange of capital through social networks is critical to locate employment, to move up from one position to a better one, or to succeed in the business, say, of selling popsicles or baked bread. In this chapter, however, I focus on family and neighborhood with regard to the recognition and exchange of social capitals. The changes that have occurred in the nature and scope of social capital reflect the transformation of the basic social field itself, and the strategies and struggles associated with different types of capital. Social capital has not only altered in its form and its usefulness, but has, to some extent, been replaced and displaced by other forms of transactions. Social capital, far from being an asset in the community as a whole as it was in the early years, has retreated behind familial walls and into the compounds of extended families. Here social capital is alive and well, but often overlooked or misrecognized by family members (as in the case of Consuelo's family and their feeling that one is often an undeserving sister). In the early days of community development, social capital was all people had, and community members used it wisely and effectively.

It is important to note how these changes have become natural and seamless as residents have moved (in terms of their own self-identity) from their previous status as squatters or, as many identified themselves, *paracaídistas* (parachutists) to their new self-identified position as urban citizens. There is also a logic that works in parallel between residents and the city status of the colonia, because as the colonia became recognized as a suburb, residents gradually took on the mantle of Oaxacan citizens: engaged and entitled.

MARGARITA

"Well, you know where we used to live in the colonia before we moved to this new place, Vista Nuevo? Well, we bought that land from Enrique Guzmán, the head of the Mesa Directiva! I got the money by participating in a *tanda* [a rotating credit group] with my family. Every fifteen days we paid 500 pesos to the tanda as a savings account. Then, it was my turn, and I heard about the lots for sale in the colonia. I bought it for 1,000 pesos. I believe that Guzmán cheated me because he promised to give me twenty meters and he only gave me seven. My husband said to let it go, and to just get busy and set up the house. We had already given Guzmán the money, and since we trusted him, we didn't get anything written down on paper. We wanted to get into our own house because we had been living with my mother-in-law for a year, and already we had five children. So, we made our first house with very light slabs of wood and a tar paper roof. We had only the first floor and I cooked with a coal stove.[1] My husband was a truck driver, and I always made his money last. So, for instance, I would use one liter of milk, four liters of rice with water, eggs and salsa with green tomatoes. That way I could feed everyone. My unmarried sister and my mother would help sometimes. They would bring me milk and clothes for the children. Also, even though my husband had 'adventures,' he did not have his second family. That came later.[2]

"I wanted to go out and get a job but I didn't know what to do with the children. Life was hard, especially because our tar paper roof leaked, and everyone slept in the same bed. I became depressed and I was always tired, but I couldn't sleep. My husband would go on a trip, and I would say to him, 'Listen, I can't stand this any more. The kids are also suffering and we are always getting wet in the rain.' 'Oh,' he would say, 'you're just exaggerating.' But as soon as he slept at home, he saw what was happening, so he asked for credit from his boss, and he put tiles on the roof and promised that he would do better with the house. So we carried on. I started to sell eggs in the colonia, because there were very few stores then. I took care of chickens and sold eggs for 10 centavos apiece. Also my neighbors and I would give each other things that we might need. I was comadre to one of my neighbors, but I would also exchange with other neighbors—we would give food and sometimes a few pesos. One of my neighbors had a small store in her house. She would bring things in from the centro. She gave me credit for food. In the colonia we all got along, until my children were grown and finished with their education.

"Here in our new colonia where we moved a long time ago [to Colonia Vista Nueva, one mile north up the highway], we get along, but we don't give anything to one another [between neighbors] because, thanks be to God, I have enough. Sometimes at my chicken stand people ask for credit, but I only give it to a few people I know. I have one neighbor who always asks me because she has troubles. Sometimes people ask for 30 or 40 pesos of chicken, like the woman who makes tortillas. So then we exchange—sometimes both goods and money. Those that receive have to give something, right?

"Right now, all of my children live around me except for two boys who live in Guadalajara. One of my sons went to the United States and returned with a lot of money. He has since lost that by going into business with a cousin—and because he was very foolish."

THIS CHAPTER EXPLORES colonia family and friendship structures. It also examines how residents, now and in the past, met daily needs through their reliance upon members of their household and their neighbors. The shape and character of this system of social relations, often very complex, altered as the settlement developed. The social capital that emerges from family and employment, typical of the latest period of development, is different than that which developed from early networks of exchange between neighbors. In the early days of the colonia, residents relied upon each other as neighbors and compadres for daily help with food, money, and child care. As most of the families were young and without a network of family ties in the city, they depended almost entirely on one another. Women created and maintained social relationships with neighbors with whom they visited each day, and on the basis of domestic services that they could offer to well-to-do compadres in the city. Each type of friendship was, in part, a relationship that was used strategically, which is not to say that such relationships were consciously entered into as strategic choices. Only the men who had stable jobs with steady incomes developed their own compadre relationships, primarily with coworkers outside of the home. Furthermore, their friendships were rarely used for domestic support, such as obtaining money for food. It is important to note that the neighborly exchanges between women were influenced by the geographical locations within the settlement, and by the position of the household in the hierarchy of the social field. In this geographical sense their lives were quite circumscribed.

Now, of course, my original informants are older. Some of their children are living in extended family compounds, while others have moved away from the colonia entirely, generally for work. Help is now centered within this extended family and seems to function in two ways. First, children living away from home send money to parents. Second, grown children and their children will daily help the grandparents who live close to them or within the same family compound. This facilitates the family safety net. In this same localized network, grown children also share goods and money with one another.

Within this general situation, I have noticed a subtle difference in behavior between grown children who are more financially well off and those who are not. Wealthier siblings tend to interact with one another through their parents and at family celebrations such as birthdays. These advantaged siblings usually do not have day-to-day contact with one another because they generally live away from the family home. This is particularly true of sons, who, unless they are having financial or marital difficulties, tend to leave family duties to their sisters and wives. This pattern of interaction raises the question of how siblings will interact with one another once their parents are no longer alive. Will the family safety net continue to function, or will another pattern emerge, different again from the two systems that went before?

Those siblings who actively help one another with basic needs have created a second form of sibling relationships; however, such supportive relationships are laced with social judgments insofar as better-off siblings will criticize other family members for not working hard enough. For instance, about Consuelo, her sister Leticia says:

Everyone in the family wants their children to study, except Consuelo. I think that the problem is the death of her husband and alcohol. She did not give enough attention to her first child. He grew up with us at home, not with Consuelo. He studied at the primary school, and then his father came to get him and he studied as an engineer. But there's a big difference between him and the other children she has. I think it's because Consuelo and her husband were not interested in the children. When kids say they don't want to go to school, that they're lazy, the parents need to teach the children how to work—to be serious and to meet their obligations. This is the authority of the parents. Most people prógress from below, but not Consuelo. She wanted to start at the top. She doesn't like hard work every day—she works, but needs a bit of glamour. She likes to go around pretty. She doesn't like to cook at home, but she doesn't have any job preparation to do anything else.

From the experiences of families who have lost their parents, I have found that the brothers and sisters who are less able to support themselves tend to congregate in their parents' family home as if their natal family is still intact. Like Consuelo, colonia residents do not recognize this pattern of family help as being central to their day-to-day survival strategies. For them, success has resulted from individual achievement and is not tied to sibling help. Even though the field of social relations and its attendant safety net has changed, many residents believe it has disappeared altogether. They continue to reference the narrative of individual success and not family help, despite the fact that each member of the extended family can receive help from others in the form of money, jobs, food, child care, and a place to stay.

Changes in the patterns of mutual help between siblings appear to be connected to three particular characteristics. The first is that residents have come to identify with the city and to see themselves as city people. This means that even though many still live in family compounds in the colonia, they are members of nucleated households supported by the earned income from both partners. Secondly, the patterns of their lives as workers has changed their daily rhythms, and thus the structure of family life. For example, the chances for a large, family-centered comida each day are disappearing, save for special occasions and some Sundays. Third, the economic situation of wealthier siblings is generally much better than that of their parents or their poorer siblings because they are not living hand-to-mouth. For all these reasons, family life and its attendant social relations have changed.

EARLY COLONIA HOUSEHOLDS AND SOCIAL RELATIONSHIPS

The basic unit of analysis throughout my years of fieldwork was the household, which often incorporated an extended family. By using the household as the basic unit of analysis, it was possible to study the different responses of individuals to general conditions in the colonia and specific changes within families. Households and their members participated in various network and support groups that overlapped the fields of politics, economics, and friendship—including the fictive kinship ties of compadrazgo. I too entered into such compadre relationships with some of my informants. These were not the more critical ties centered on baptism or marriage, but the lesser ties created at minor events, such as being a comadre of a birthday or rosary, which simply meant that as Catholics we went to the local cathedral, said a prayer at the altar, and the bond was sealed. Frankly, I am not so sure that being a Catholic would even have been necessary. The critical point of making our relationships formal was the desire of both parties to establish that connection. So while these connections were not the critical compadre relationships, such ties were a ritualized way of ensuring a closer friendship that allowed a sharing of resources and permitted us to ask one another for help. In this way we each were being strategic, sharing a variety of capitals.

In the early days of Colonia Hermosa, all household economies relied upon such networks between neighbors and local people. Also, these social connections and the formation of social capital gained by way of their networks helped residents form a community. It is crucial to keep these important social networks in mind as one learns about the development of households in the colonia: how people came to the colonia, and how they began to build their lives there.

In the late 1990s, the colonia-based networks had disappeared in favor of strategies built upon the income of grown children, along with alliances developed through sibling connections. This is an enormous shift in the kinds of mechanisms by which families survive. Acknowledging that this type of shift in the field of social capital and social relations does take place is an essential step for all those who wish to understand more clearly the impact of developing economies on family life. In this instance, community ties weaken, even though family ties remain strong, especially when a parent is still involved at the center of the household. The conclusion to be drawn here is one that reminds us of the importance of help from consanguineal family relations, and the decreasing importance of help from neighbors, friends, and compadres as parents now rely more and more on their own grown children.

DAILY SURVIVAL AND ECONOMIC COOPERATION: SINGLE MOTHERS

TERESA: A DREAM OF ROMANCE

In 1969, Teresa was working with her mother, Elena, and her sister Rosa in the home of a wealthy family. She had given birth to two children by one of the younger sons of the family. From 1969 to 1974, she repeatedly told me that he acknowledged the children as his own, sent her child support (which often did not arrive), and would someday live with her as her husband. When Teresa began her relationship with this man, she was fourteen years old; when I met her, she was seventeen. She felt that even if her free-union husband had a first marriage (which he eventually did), that he would take her as a "second wife" and support her and the children for life. What was clear to me at the time was how desperate she felt—that she longed for a life with some ease, not to mention material goods such as clothes and furniture. To succeed in her goals, she was pinning her hopes on this particular man to rescue her from the more wearisome life that she saw stretching out before her.

Teresa's two children were her obvious link to the wealthy family and their son, but her actual day-to-day support came from her sisters, her mother, and her brother-in-law, who constructed her house. But this practical support she only vaguely acknowledged. She had set her sights on something else: becoming a second wife to a wealthy man. She expected support from an imagined future, which in some important ways mirrors Consuelo's imagined life with her first husband, Roberto.

I remember, during the first few years of my fieldwork, Teresa telling me how her story would end happily. We would be sitting in her two-room house, which she shared with her mother and brother. Sometimes we would drink a cup of Nescafé together; usually I brought sweet bread to eat, and she would discuss her life, and her belief that soon she would no longer have to work, but would be supported by her lover, and perhaps would be able to afford a nicer house in the colonia.

One side of her house was the hillside itself, so it was dirt and stone. The house had been built from wattle and daub (bamboo and mud) and had a tar paper roof and a pounded dirt floor. There was no separate cook shack, so meals were prepared on a two-burner kerosene stove inside the house. The room was dark, having no windows, and it smelled of cooking oil and unwashed bed linen. To the left of the wooden door was one bed where she and her children slept. In the middle of the room was an unfinished wooden table and chairs purchased either from the central market or from one of the door-to-door vendors. They also had a wooden chest and an assortment of storage baskets, some lying on top of the old wooden chest. In the second room were two beds where Elena and Teresa's younger brother slept. The walls of the house were decorated with calendars, a few religious pictures, and a small altar with votive candles. The only appliances were two radios. The beds and the radios were gifts from Teresa's lover. Although Teresa had twelve dresses (more clothes than most of my informants), five had been purchased with time payments from door-to-door vendors. It was in this very humble home that we would sit discussing Teresa's life and dreams.

In the 1970s, as a twenty-something, Teresa had a third child by another man and created yet another dream of leaving her life of poverty behind. Since that time, she has had five more children with a series of men. Thus, over the years, while she did maintain her home and her children without a permanent relationship with a man, she continued to live her life within the ideological and emotional boundaries of a nuclear family—albeit a dream one. In this way, her female-centered household contrasts sharply with that of Aída, who chose to live without a male partner and decided instead to pin her future dreams on what she felt was the less risky future of her own son's education and his potential earning power in the job market. In actuality, Teresa's support has always come from her immediate family, including her children, who were able to find work and share their income with her.

By the late 1990s, Teresa was working in a hotel as a maid. Her children have worked in various jobs, including as a mechanic, a receptionist in a hotel, and a laborer in a milk factory. One traveled to the United States (without papers) to look for work and, as his cousin explained, for some excitement. Nearly fifty years old by the year 2000, Teresa then had two daughters continuing to live at home. She and her sisters now live in another colonia, and her house is up the street from that of her sister Isabel. Her mother, Elena, and her sister Rosa also live close by. So, while the family no longer lives in a compound, they are neighbors, and they continue to depend on each other.

AÍDA: PLANNING THROUGH EDUCATION

Aída, though impoverished, orchestrated an economic plan in the early days of living in Colonia Hermosa. Her eldest son, Santiago, was educated with her backing, and he supported himself through outside work as an apprentice to an electrician. This schooling was an investment in the future, and was calculated and rigorous. All of Aída's resources were directed toward day-to-day survival and making sure her son would be able to find a steady job. What is interesting is that her plans included only her eldest child. Her two younger sons did not have such expectations placed upon them, nor were they given any responsibility for the family's future—nor, in later years, did they take such responsibility upon themselves. It is clear that Aída's eldest son took on the role of the father, as he was continuing to do in the year 2000, even though he had his own wife and family. Describing Santiago, his youngest brother, Alejandro, says:

> To me he was my father. I always respected him. He had a lot of responsibility, and he would also discipline us; sometimes he would hit us. At night, when he got home from work or school, maybe around six at night, and my brother Gustavo and I would be in the street playing—which he didn't want us to do—he wanted us to do homework or to work—we'd go home running so he wouldn't get angry.

In addition to help from her oldest son, Aída benefited from sharing food, as well as small amounts of money, with her neighbors, especially her compadres who lived on the dirt road above her house. This couple had helped her dig out of her first house, which collapsed under mud in the ravine. They not only helped her with daily loans, but they also sold her handmade tortillas in their store and encouraged her to seek child support from her husband by attaching his wages. This was possible because he had acknowledged her two younger boys as his children, and because he was employed by a federal agency. Since Aída and her younger sons have moved to a colonia across town, she is supported by whichever son lives with her in the house and land supplied by Santiago. As mentioned earlier, Gustavo (the middle son) and Alejandro share a second house that they bought with their share of the money from the sale of their house in the colonia. Every so often, the younger brothers and their families change houses: one to Alejandro's place, and the other to Santiago's house, where Aída lives. In return, Aída helps with their children, laundry, and cooking. Thus nowadays Aída rarely needs help from others except from her sons. Her interaction with neighbors is structured by a government-assisted group for the elderly. Aída meets with the group a few times a month to talk, sew, and knit. They are given a stipend for coffee, beans, and bread. What is very different from her former interaction with her neighbors in Colonia Hermosa is that their time is structured, and no neighborly help occurs within the group. Aída seems to take advice only from her eldest son, who pays for her health benefits and helps with other expenses when she cannot meet them. Of this, she says:

> Life in this [new] colonia is really different. . . . Here there aren't people like that [who would help one another]. There is an elderly woman, also a neighbor, who we give food to because, poor thing, she has no family to help her. The person who I have the most confidence in is the woman who lives here in front, the one who has the telephone. So if we need something from the store and for the moment we don't have money, she will help, and when Alejandro has money, he will pay her. So she has loaned me money [this is always only a matter of a few pesos] or goods, and I will give her loans also. This is the only family I do this with. It would be better to get loans from Santiago and Alicia, but they don't live close. If they did, it would be better with them.

As noted above, there can be problems when family members consistently lend money to one another; however, Aída commented that

Santiago "isn't bothered by this. He prefers us to come to him. But sometimes it bothers Alejandro, because at his age he doesn't like to feel like a child."

In addition to providing his mother with a house, Santiago is often called upon for other types of help. For instance, as mentioned earlier, over the last six years or so the family had come together with Aída's brother and mother before the grandmother passed away. Both were given money for health care by Santiago, which is very generous of him given that they took no part in his upbringing. His generosity is a clear indication of his respect for his mother's wishes. I asked Aída and Alejandro to tell me about their trip to see his grandmother. I mentioned that I had remembered that Aída's mother was very angry and not kind to Aída when she was young. Aída's theory about her mother's early behavior, as mentioned previously, is that since she had to work like a man or do men's work in the fields in order to keep her house, she developed the character of a man and became hardened and mean. Using folk ideas of gender-specific behavior, she responded:

> But of course a woman is not the same as a man. So what happened was that something happened to her womb. It almost turned inside out. This is why she was not normal. But in the hospital they cured her.
>
> Anyway, the day came when my brother called me by telephone and said that Mamá is very bad. He didn't want me to come there, but to send him money. Santiago had finished studying and was working, so he sent money to help. He sent money from April to October to his uncle which was supposed to help care for my mother, as he lived with my mother. Santiago gathered 3,000 pesos and my mother had an operation. My brother did not have any money because his wife had divorced him. His three daughters went with his wife, and they needed all his money and his house. He was left with nothing. Before, he worked in a restaurant, but now he is much too old to work. He didn't go to school. Neither of us went to school.

NEIGHBORHOOD WOMEN: A LANDSCAPE FOR SUPPORT

MARGARITA

By the late 1990s, Margarita's children were grown up and had, together, created a family business that was successful for eight years. Since the business had closed, she and her children had continued to live in close

FIGURE 6.1. Margarita (*center*) with three of her children and a grandson, 2000

proximity and often helped one another with gifts of food, child care, and work; however, each now has his or her own business or work, and all of them have separate families except the two unmarried brothers. For Margarita, this is where the real success of her family and life is located: working together to create a foundation upon which the family could take advantage of educational opportunities and increased financial stability so that her grandchildren could grow up, as cousins, together.

Margarita's social relationships now, as in the late 1960s and early 1970s, are completely separate from those of her husband, who is usually not with her. At one time he was always working, driving first-class trucks to and from Mexico City. He would spend many days with his second family. He spent very little time with Margarita and their children, which was his first family, or with his compadres. There was one year (1970–1971) that they had no fiestas, or celebrations, with their friends and relatives, which is very unusual for colonia families. Margarita's husband has been separated from her now for some years and lives with another woman, although he still visits Margarita and begs, she says, to be taken back. Well over her hurt at his perfidy, she finds this an amusing turn of events and feels empowered by her situation: she has her own business, selling chickens down the street from her house in a small, wooden street-front stall. Most of her grown children are close by, and she has taken over the family home, so she is no longer dependent in any way upon her husband. As outlined earlier, Margarita used to rely heavily on her friends and relatives for help to meet the weekly needs of her family, as well as for simple emotional support and a social life apart from her life with her husband. When her several children were young, she was very lonely and extremely upset that her husband had mistresses, and that he finally formed a second family. Other women in the colonia were not particularly sympathetic to her plight, although she was valued as a friend. They felt that she was supported well economically, and that her husband was doing his duty to her and to her children. In common with other women who were not considered wealthy but in the regular or poor strata of the colonia,[3] Margarita would see her friends and neighbors every day. They were all poorer than she, and together they exchanged food, money, and labor. Usually it was Margarita, because of her better financial position, who offered food and money, although someone like María (Consuelo's mother) would bring her food if she were cooking something special to sell.

In the wider city of Oaxaca, Margarita had two important comadres, one of whom was a doctor. She related to me that she felt quite equal to her, and she never seemed embarrassed or worried that the comadre would get tired of Margarita asking for help. This attitude is not one that was shared by other colonia women who had doctors as comadres. Unlike them, however, Margarita had never worked for her comadre as a cook, nor did she do her laundry. Both she and her sister had married working-class men with steady employment and incomes that allowed them to indulge in makeup, shopping for clothes, and visits to the hairdresser. Since she and her children were covered by health insurance through her husband's job, she was not totally dependent upon the charity of her comadre. This is probably one of the most important differences between Margarita and her neighbors: the fact that health care was not reliant on the good will of her patron-client relationships.

Margarita's other comadre was a primary school teacher whom she had met when her family moved to the city many years ago. They are friends, and not involved in a patron-client relationship. They exchange small gifts and food, but the relationship is not used for daily support. In the early 1970s, if there was an emergency and if her family could not help her, Margarita told me that she would turn to these comadres rather than to her colonia friends. The reasons for using this strategy, she said, had to do with her colonia friends' lack of resources, and the fact that her Oaxacan comadres more closely resembled Margarita and her lifestyle. Clearly she was seeking to identify with the class dispositions and habitus of her comadres, not with that of the colonia residents. Now, of course, Margarita is even more self-contained. She needs only herself and her children.

BERTA

Berta Nava's friends in Colonia Hermosa lived in houses that were clustered around her own home. Because her husband earned a steady income as a second-class bus driver, and because they had only two children, Berta did not have to work to help support the family, even though they were very poor and lived in only one room of a larger house that was rented to another family. She was never a popular woman, and despite her colonia friendships, she had no compadres there, which is quite a striking difference. All of her compadres lived in the city, and all of her kin lived in a highland mestizo village. Her husband's relatives lived in Oaxaca, but she did not get along with them. Berta struck people as being too opinionated, as being an untrustworthy gossip, rather too grouchy, and generally too critical of the people around her. Nevertheless, her neighbors did exchange goods and gossip with her.

The family itself owned nothing, which was unusual in Colonia Hermosa. Instead they rented a room in one of Guzmán's houses, and they used a cook shack. After one family vacated the house, my husband and I lived in it. We were separated from Berta and her family by a kitchen door. Her family had very little furniture and had neither economic nor cultural capital. Since they played no part in colonia public life, and since they were not generous to their neighbors, they also lacked symbolic capital. Berta's husband would get drunk every Sunday and did not help with the tequio. This sort of behavior was disapproved of by many colonia families and was seen as an obvious mark of social failure, as was also the case with María's husband, Alfredo. Berta's networks of friends—whom she called *amistades*, or acquaintances, and not friends—were those neighbors who lived close to her. With these women she exchanged food, medical advice, medicine, and child care. She also helped one particular woman friend, Angela, with her laundry job, because she felt that her friend's daughter Reyna was too selfish to help her mother. Berta was often to be seen standing in the middle of the path with her youngest child wrapped in her black and grey rebozo, held against her hip while she gossiped with her neighbors. Because she had no real kin ties, she depended on her friends for support and goods. Usually these women exchanged their friendship and food gifts for the goods she had available, such as tortillas, fruit, labor, and child care.

Berta had two favorite comadres in town whom she visited on a regular basis. One was the wife of a bus driver who worked for the same company as her husband, and the other was the wife of a school-teacher. Like Margarita, Berta saw her comadres as friends rather than seeing herself as being in a patron-client relationship. In times of emotional stress, Berta would confide in these women, but they did not help her directly with daily economic activities. Never realizing the general colonia opinion of her or her husband, she put herself above the women in the colonia and rarely confided in them. As I never met her city compadres, I can not say if her feelings for these women were reciprocated.

After Berta's husband died in the late 1980s, she and her children returned home to her highland village—or so everyone said. They also said that she died in the 1990s after having suffered with cancer. Nowadays the one room they lived in has been incorporated back into the larger house structure, and Enrique Guzmán's nephew lives there with his family. Neighbors say that he is a taxi driver, but that they do not interact with him or his family.

REYNA

Reyna lived next to Berta and to Margarita. Other than her mother and sister, who also lived in the colonia, these women were her only friends. Between 1969 and 1974, all of her compadres were living in Oaxaca city and had been introduced to her through her husband's workplace. These were special circumstances, as most husbands do not choose or negotiate most compadre relationships in the colonia. Reyna's husband, Humberto, drove a delivery truck for a soft drink bottling company, which is considered to be a very good job, providing a steady income and health benefits through the Social Security Hospital. What is distinctive is that Reyna was the only woman in the group who maintained relationships with compadres that she had not chosen herself. Her husband dominated these relationships, and they were all made through his place of work. He also decided which fiestas were celebrated and which guests were to be invited. Since her husband had a steady income and health insurance, they were less likely to turn to compadres for help in emergencies, but no doubt his compadres were helpful to him at their place of work.

When I was her neighbor, Reyna was twenty-two years old and had three small children. She lived directly across from my bedroom on the other side of the pathway going up the hill. Although she did not leave home in order to work, she did enjoy going to Oaxaca or just walking around the colonia to visit her mother, Angela. If her mother or sister were not available to help, she would ask Berta to stay with her children while she went off on some errand. Although Berta would visit Reyna's house, Reyna would not go to Berta's house, because she said it was "inconvenient." Her hesitancy was actually due to the disgraceful binge drinking of Berta's husband on the weekends, and because of the poor surroundings of Berta's house. Such an insult infuriated Berta, but she nonetheless maintained their relationship. Reyna rarely asked Margarita to mind her children, although she would visit Margarita in her home. In fact, Margarita almost never visited Reyna's home, which is a clear indication of their relative positions in the social field.

Reyna exchanged money, food, child care, and clothes with her mother and sister. Between them, Reyna, her mother, and her sister Luz created something closer to friendships than a hierarchical relationship between a mother and her daughter, or between an older and younger sister. They are an example of a common pattern between mothers and their adult daughters, not unlike María and her daughters. It was only because of daily emergencies that Reyna would turn to her mother, sister, Berta, or Margarita. The families of Reyna and Berta both remained aloof from community work, much like María's household but quite different from Isabel's family or Aída's and even Margarita's family.

One might imagine that Reyna and Berta's positions in the social field would have also been comparable. After all, both husbands earned a weekly wage, both had access to health care from insurance, and they both had only two children. That, however, is where the similarities ended. Berta sat on the ground in the doorway of her one room, whereas Reyna sat on a chair in her patio in front of her three-room house. Berta had a ramshackle shack for cooking, while Reyna had a concrete cook shack separate from the house. Berta had very little furniture, while Reyna had two beds, a table, and chairs. Most important were the differences in their bodily postures, attitudes, and expectations. Reyna's husband had the dispositions of the city; with his steady job and good income, he was also formal and withdrawn in his manner. This passed as a demonstration of his social position in colonia society. In sharp contrast, Berta's husband did not shave or change his clothes all weekend, as he only slept and drank. Between Reyna and Berta there were huge differences in levels of social capital: as far as Reyna was concerned, these were very clear, and from her point of view such differences provided the structure for her relationship with Berta.

In 2000 Reyna and her family were still living in Colonia Hermosa, but her house had been remodeled and now has brick covering the white concrete of thirty years ago. They have added on a second story and now have modern indoor kitchen, so they no longer use the cook shack. They also have a five-foot-high brick wall around their yard, which allows them a private patio. Reyna's son, now grown, is a taxi driver. He continues to live with his parents in their compound, along with his young wife and family.

MARÍA

María, like most women in the colonia, was solely responsible for establishing the social relationships upon which her family would depend for day-to-day survival. Between 1968 and 1974, she had developed a close circle of friends who lived nearby and with whom she talked every day. She also had two compadres in town who were medical practitioners, and other compadres on the coast of Oaxaca whom she would visit two or three times a year when she was selling clothes village to village or going on a pilgrimage to the Virgin of Juquila. Her kin ties were limited to her mother-in-law and to the husband and child of her daughter, who later died. Interestingly, these particular relations did not feature in her life at all after her daughter died, not even her grandson. María claimed that she and her husband were still close to their son-in-law, and that he visited three or four times a year with their grandson, but over my years working with this family, I have never met him, nor did I ever see any evidence that he and the grandson had actually visited. Also, I was never made aware of any important exchanges between the two families.

One of María's friends and, later, comadres was Margarita. They would visit daily since they lived across the footpath from one another, and they would exchange small amounts of money, food, and child care.[4] The flow of goods generally moved from Margarita's more organized household to María's less organized household. However, as friends, they were mutually supportive in times of trouble. Above María's house lived the García and Portillo families. Like María and Alfredo, these families were also considered very poor by colonia residents, but they maintained a high level of social capital. They did not carry the stigma of drinking too much, or of being responsible for coarse behavior, as did María and Alfredo. The women in these families loaned María tortillas, masa (ground corn flour), and other food when her own supplies were low. Another neighbor, Berta, would stop and chat each day, although they both would gossip about each other. Berta thought María's family was crude, while María though Berta to be pretentious, with middle-class aspirations to which she had no right.

Both of their husbands had serious problems with weekend binge drinking. When I lived in the colonia, Consuelo was a constant visitor to the house, as were some of her siblings. From this vantage point I was able to see the comings and goings of María and her neighbors, and I became part of their ladies' gossip network.

María's compadres in town included a married couple who practiced medicine and a woman who was a *curandera*, or traditional folk healer. María always used both types of medicine for family illnesses, so these networks were practical as well as critical in helping to keep her family healthy. The maintenance of family health was generally thought to be gender-specific to women. The relationship between María and the medical doctors was a classical patron-client relationship. In exchange for medical help and loans of money from the doctor, María would do domestic work, such as cooking a fiesta meal or doing the family laundry. The relationship that María had with the curandera was not quite so formal, and they would often visit one another simply as friends.

Before her death in the mid-1970s, María's mother-in-law visited the colonia about once a month to see her son and grandchildren. She always appeared to hate María, although that didn't keep her from accepting the food and hospitality that was offered. She would give nothing in return and was never asked for help by either María or Alfredo. Whenever María and Consuelo made trips to sell clothes and other items, or when they were making a pilgrimage to the Virgin of Juquila, María would visit her compadres who lived on the coast of Oaxaca. They would offer food and lodging, and would help María to buy fruit to take back to sell. The only other supportive relationship that María had was with her daughter Consuelo and, as they grew older, her other daughters. Theirs was a relationship of friendship and constant mutual support consisting of the provision of money, food, and family care. Consuelo provided María and her family with money, appliances, and other help when she was young and working in the pharmacy, and María would help Consuelo with child care, laundry, and cooked food. Basically, Consuelo earned money *outside* of the home, and María would produce goods *inside* the home. Although Consuelo's in-laws (by her first husband) lived in the colonia, there had been no contact between the families, neither before nor since the divorce. As mentioned in Chapter 3, this was because María and Alfredo had little status, prestige, or economic capital. In contrast, the parents of Consuelo's first husband were rural schoolteachers and had pretensions of being better than most of the other colonia residents.

LETICIA

Of her working life, Leticia, María's second eldest daughter, says that at age fourteen, as she was finishing primary school, her family was so poor that they did not have enough to eat. She says:

> My mother did not encourage me to go and finish school. She thought, born poor, die poor. She always wanted me to work. I helped her to sell enchiladas, and to sell other things here in the colonia, house to house, washing clothes and ironing, ever since I was eight or nine years old. So, that's why I was always thinking about work and making money.
>
> I began working outside the house. I started in a business at a supermarket for a Oaxacan family. There I worked for seven years. They treated me well. Then, to progress a little more, I worked in a wine and liquor company. I worked there for three years. Then I went to another store. I was the chief cashier, and I had really good work there for five years. I was really helping my family a lot. I was helping my brothers with their studies, as well as my younger sisters and youngest brother, Moises. And that's how we progressed, thanks to God, little by little. . . . No one helped Consuelo or me. No one else in the family. Thank goodness they all have good jobs, but what they have is only for them. They don't help the rest of us out very much.
>
> When I was a girl, what happened here in the colonia was that everyone helped one another. Everyone was very humble. We would give a bit of this comida, or tortillas, or water to wash. Now? Well, now that I have no need, we all have enough. The reality is that I, at least, am *amistades* [acquaintances] with everyone. We are friendly with everyone. Here in the colonia there are always problems between people—gossip and whatever—but with us there is none. Because we have suffered so much as youngsters, I give to anyone who asks, even if I don't eat. Sometimes people come by to beg—the new people from the top of the hill. I save my leftovers in the refrigerator.

ISABEL

During the first two decades of their lives in Colonia Hermosa, Isabel and her husband, Arturo, were characterized by other residents as being a poor family. This characterization was based on their ethnic background as indigenous Mazatec (Arturo) and Zapotec (Isabel) migrants, as well as on their jobs and dispositions, which ensured that they would carry themselves in a very humble manner around those in the Mesa Directiva. They first lived in the second section of the colonia, high up the hillside.

During my fieldtrips to Oaxaca in the late 1960s and again in the late 1990s, I talked to Isabel and Arturo about their residential compound and the exchange relationships between the family members who shared it. The networks that connected this household with others, and which helped support them, were made up of compadres within and beyond the colonia, as well as immediate kin and friends in the colonia. The most influential compadre relationships that Isabel and Arturo had were with his employers, who owned an ice cream factory; with Isabel's previous employers, who were city lawyers; with the Valdovia family, who were rather high-ranking in the colonia's Mesa Directiva; and with Enrique Guzmán, who was at one time the colonia's political leader. Isabel and Arturo established ties with Valdovia and Guzmán by becoming part of their political faction in the colonia.

From their compadres in the city, they would borrow money for emergencies, and Isabel would work for them by doing laundry or cooking. When a bus on a Oaxacan street killed Arturo's father, they went to both sets of city compadres for funeral money and advice about prosecuting the driver. In the end, instead of prosecuting, Arturo took the advice of the diviner from his Mazatec village, who told him to leave retribution to God and to carry on with his own life.

Their relationships with their colonia compadres are more complicated. Isabel often worked for Sra. Valdovia, making clothes for her market stand. But in return for their help, the Valdovias received political support from the family in the tequio and felt entitled to call upon both Arturo and Isabel to help with any household jobs. They had a similar relationship with the family of Enrique Guzmán. Isabel and Arturo were always available to help his mother with anything that needed to be done around the house.

Isabel once remarked to me that "people like her own family" did not get the opportunities that people like the Valdovias and Guzmáns had available to them. This remark came after Isabel's request to set up a tortilla vending space outside the new colonia market that started in the 1970s was rejected by others in the hierarchy of the Mesa Directiva. The colonos who started the market actually bought into rights to the space and invested in formal vending booths. This group did not want others out on the street selling their wares informally at the same time, despite the fact that many of the rejected vendors had worked for the Mesa Directiva and had compadre relationships with them. Thus was created a very clear divide between those who could afford the initial outlay of cash for the market stalls, and those who needed to sell on the street. Finally, Isabel was allowed to sell tortillas at the market as the pressure from other colonia residents to sell their items overpowered the initial group.

The main political actor in the colonia, Enrique Guzmán, also received political support from the family of Isabel and Arturo in exchange for money and advice. He was another of their compadres. From his vantage point, Isabel and Arturo were completely unimportant because of their poverty, their ethnicity, and their corresponding lack of economic, social, and symbolic capital. Whenever their names came up in conversation, he had to be reminded of who they were. As a result, they had no position in the field of colonia social relationships at all, except among their immediate neighbors. All of their compadre relationships were of a patron-client type.

A final comadre that Isabel and Arturo depended upon was a local healer. The woman was a friend of Isabel's as well as a comadre, and they often sought her help in treating serious illnesses. This relationship was much more of a collegial one, as was the one between María and her comadre who was also a curandera. Isabel also had three friends who lived in her area of Colonia Hermosa (second section, upper half) and with whom she maintained exchange relationships. They would help each other on a daily basis with their housework while they gossiped. They would also cook for each other when there was a special event, and bring parcels back from town for one another. Because they all lived high up on the hill in the second section of the colonia, it was truly a burden as well as an act of friendship to carry things up for their neighbors.

By 2000, Isabel and Arturo no longer appeared or behaved like people who feel that they do not belong in the city. Since their earlier days in Colonia Hermosa, they have moved farther down the highway to another colonia. Today they own their own business and live in a compound with their grown children and their families. They are justly proud that their sons and daughter have all completed at least primary school (which includes grades 1–6) and that they all have jobs that provide for themselves and their extended family in the compound. Although Isabel's mother and sisters still live close to them, having themselves vacated their older houses in Colonia Hermosa, they do not visit each day, nor do Isabel and Arturo exchange much help with them. They, like other families, now rely upon their children for daily support and company.

One of the interesting topics that we discussed when I first saw Isabel and Arturo after so many years of separation was their native languages. Arturo and his brother continue to speak to one another in Mazatec, but none of their children are fluent. They do, however, return to the original pueblos of both Isabel and Arturo, usually three or four times a year. Even though they still had land interests in each pueblo, they self-identify as Oaxacan city residents, not their former pueblos, and not as indigenous Mazatec and Zapotec. When I asked the children if they identify with their parents' natal villages, they said no, and, in fact, they denied having any feeling that they had lost something in their parents' transition from rural to urban residency. Instead they were focusing on their lives in Oaxaca and beyond, speaking only Spanish, and not identifying much with their familial ties to rural areas or their indigenous heritage.

Both Isabel and Arturo were very proud of the fact that they are seen to be social leaders, and carriers of symbolic and cultural capital, in their new colonia. As their standard of living has risen, their dispositions have changed: they are more outgoing and forthright in their manner of speaking. Also, they have grown children who can help to support them in their new position in colonia society. An important part of their social life is the busy Christmas season, when they participate in posadas and host their neighbors for the posada meals. They often spoke about how many friends they have in their new colonia. They say that they do not miss their neighbors in Colonia Hermosa; in fact, they miss nothing about their lives there, except that Arturo misses his land and his pig, so he visits them often, staying in the little house he built there for himself.

THE COLONIA WEALTHY

THE GUZMÁN FAMILY

Like Isabel and Arturo, other Colonia Hermosa residents took over a large block of land so that the larger family group would be able to live close together, as in a rural village setting, even though they migrated from Puebla, which is not a rural village. Enrique Guzmán, the leader of the Mesa Directiva, built residences for his sister and her son, as well as another for his brother, his mother, and himself before he married. Guzmán was one of the wealthiest colonia residents. One indication of his social standing is the fact that the family built their own businesses in the colonia, which clearly demonstrates that they had capital to invest before they arrived. This they accomplished through the work and incomes of the three adult siblings, who pooled their money to support the family. This is now a common pattern among other families, but it did not exist as a strategy in the first two decades of Colonia Hermosa because most families had young children. In this way the Guzmán family was ahead of the game.

The first colonia business that Enrique Guzmán started was to sell house lots to other residents, even though it later became clear that he had no clear title to the land. He had simply bought parcels from the local schoolteacher, who alleged that he had title to the land but who was later jailed for fraud. Nevertheless, in spite of the shaky legal ground for these transactions, the business succeeded. The family also created other enterprises, such as a bath house and a store which sold, among other things, kerosene for the ubiquitous two-burner stoves. They also built a large warehouse in the hope of having a successful CONASUPO[5] in the community. For this family, the land in the colonia was used not only for housing, but also for economic investment. In addition, both Guzmán and his brother were employed at a local radio station. Guzmán became a local announcer, and his brother drove a small car with a large loudspeaker on top to advertise events and products. Later, according to some informants, Guzmán became a representative in local state government, or at least held a position in the local government.

The Guzmáns' strategy of land use demonstrates that the family compound approach was a sensible model to follow, and these compounds later became an important part of the local Colonia Hermosa neighborhood. Particular families had different strategic uses for the land that they either bought or simply took as squatters. Economic necessity and the pressure of the city, coupled with a transformation of village sensibilities, all led to a different type of productive use of the urban land, and to the need for new social practices in the city. For instance, consider the benefits of families living in the same compound as opposed to different units in a *vecindad*, an inner-city apartment complex. There are clearly enormous social benefits to new migrants who stay with family in the colonia until they are able to create their own city space. All kinds of information, forms of informal knowledge, social contacts, and leads for work, not to mention the material conditions of support—all of these are available in such a setting. During the late 1970s the city offered what they considered to be low-cost housing to settlers such as those in Colonia Hermosa. Streets, lights, water, and sewage connections were part of the package. But such housing did not prove popular to my informants, for as they pointed out, they would have had to pay rent or a mortgage, and they would have had to buy more furniture to fill a house with three or four bedrooms! This just was not a good deal for them.

It is also clear from the way many colonia residents have organized kin networks that they do not visualize themselves as living in nuclear families, as some middle-class Mexican families do, except when they themselves have sufficient income to live in separate, nucleated households. These new conditions might then allow them to take on the general appearance of middle-class life, as Consuelo's sisters and Margarita's children have. Commonly, Colonia Hermosa families continue to live together within compounds, as some of Isabel and Arturo's children have continued to do. They may do this without necessarily supporting each other financially. Thus the family group owns the land and houses, avoiding rent and mortgage, but at the same time tries to maintain a series of nucleated households. The women in these households may still share food and child care, but commonly they do not offer each other financial help, as Consuelo's sisters help her. Having their own place in the city, and having been given legal title to land and property, has probably been the most beneficial action for the early colonia residents. It allowed some to move forward from a position of subproletariat along the trajectory to become part of the working class.

By the year 2000, the original Guzmán compound looked vastly different than it did in the late 1960s and 1970s. First, the original compound, which had housed the two brothers and their mother, had been converted into a large, two-story hotel. Guzmán was living there alone, as his wife had divorced him and taken the children to their city home. Guzmán still had rights to the water-bottling company (brought to the family by his wife), which was being run by his children. Guzmán's sister was continuing to live in her original house, which had backed onto the property of the bath houses that she had helped to run for the family. The bath houses are now gone, sold to develop more housing and outbuildings for the hotel. However, the sister was continuing to maintain a small store in her home. Her son, now grown, is a taxi driver, and has moved into another of Guzmán's houses up the main road into the colonia. This was the house that I rented many years ago, and which my husband and I shared with Berta and her family. When I last was in Oaxaca, in 2000, I was unable to see Enrique Guzmán as he was extremely ill, and the colonia was full of stories that he was expected to die very soon.

THE SÁNCHEZ FAMILY

Within the colonia, both the Sánchez and the Valdovia families were considered by their neighbors to be among the wealthy residents. In the late 1960s and early 1970s, the head of the Sánchez family, Miguel, was employed in the city as a plumber. Miguel is a short, stocky man with a very youthful face and a rather charming manner. He is so charming, in fact, that in the 1980s, after his wife, Gloria, died, Miguel ran off with his son's young wife. They still live together in town.

Gloria had what might be termed a "larger than life" personality that matched her physical form, and she was an amazing but sometimes overwhelming person. She had an easy laugh; she was garrulous, bossy, and always had something to say, as well as new schemes for making money. She worked from home making food to sell, working with metal to make the small charcoal stoves that everyone used, and sewing clothes to sell in the Oaxacan market stalls of her friends. Since she had spent much of her adolescence in Oaxaca, she had several contacts there. When the Mesa Directiva set up their local market, she bought into a stall and sold clothes and, now and then, food. Gloria was very close to her father and to her two married sisters, one of whom, Esperanza, matched her in wit and nearly in girth. They had all arrived in the colonia together and continued to live there. Except for Gloria and her father, who are now deceased, the family is still anchored in Colonia Hermosa. In fact, Gloria's eldest daughter, Laura, now sits in her little storefront tienda, looking just like Gloria herself, selling her food, presiding over her own family and those of her sisters, who still live in the compound, now fenced off from what continues to be the colonia's main street.

Miguel and Gloria, along with her two sisters and her father, came to Colonia Hermosa from inner-city slums after hearing the fraudulent schoolteacher/developer's advertisements about lots on the local radio. Between family members there was not an article of clothing, a piece of food, or any other sort of support or money that was not open for use between them. Their children would stay in each other's homes for days at a time.

The family quickly became associates of Enrique Guzmán and part of the Mesa Directiva. They also established compadre ties with their cohort on the Mesa Directiva, as well as with Guzmán and his mother. In the city they had compadre relationships with a patrón from Miguel's workplace, and with a few women who worked in the central market who were particular friends of Gloria's. Miguel's patrón would lend the family money in exchange for labor. In the colonia, the most important compadre relationship that Gloria had was with a shopkeeper who extended credit to her each week. Because Gloria sometimes sold cooked food in her market stall, both she and the shopkeeper gained from the credit that he allowed her; this constituted a form of what anthropologists call a collegial dyad.

But while the Sánchez family kept a high profile in the colonia, especially with regard to their work on the Mesa Directiva and their association with Sr. Guzmán, colonia residents tended to characterize the family as being very low class in their manner and dispositions — as no different than slum residents, which was quite a slur on their name. The family was thought to be coarse. This characterization was extended to Gloria's sister Esperanza and to her father, who was said to always "have a new woman around." Their language was generally thought to be vulgar in the extreme, and their dress and housekeeping were sloppy and dirty. These were the judgments voiced by residents with what might be termed more middle-class aspirations, and who were often irritated that the Sánchez family was so close to the power of the Guzmán family, and yet *so unsuitable* for this position of respect and power!

The consequences of this characterization were very real. They shaped the interaction between the Sánchez and the Valdovia family, because the Sánchezes were placed in a subordinate position. Therefore, all visiting between the two took place at colonia events or in the Valdovia house — never on the Sánchez property, which was considered even by their compadres, the Valdovias, to be unhygienic. With regard to their mutually beneficial relationship, exchanges of labor and political support went from the Sánchezes to the Valdovias. From the Valdovias came help in organizing the first market stalls, money when a Sánchez child was very ill, and the offer of odd jobs to the larger Sánchez family and children when they might need work. With regard to the Sánchezes' compadre relationship to Guzmán and his mother, these ties were even more distant and followed the structure of a traditional patron-client relationship. Miguel and Gloria gave political support to Guzmán, visited his mother, and did small jobs for her. In return, they received some measure of respectability and the social kudos of helping with major colonia fiestas. Rarely did they ask the Guzmán family for money or paid work.

Gloria had a few special compadres in town, but what she did not seem to have were friendship ties. Except for exchanges between family members, the Sánchez family did not give or receive exchanges or support from any neighbors or friends in the colonia, save through their compadre ties to the Valdovias and to Guzmán. Their social relationships were confined to family or to formal, city-based compadre ties.

THE VALDOVIA FAMILY

The Valdovias were considered by colonia residents to be wealthy, but of a higher status than the Sánchezes because of their quieter and more polite dispositions, and because they often would contract out labor to local women who would sew clothes for their market stall. Thus they were seen as patrons to a variety of women who needed work at home. They were not beloved by colonia residents, however, and in fact many people did not like them because of what they felt was their superior attitude. In the field of Colonia Hermosa's social relationships, such self-regard was not admired, but disrespected; however, colonia residents did respect their wealth, and their connections to the Mesa Directiva and Guzmán. Consequently, their behavior toward the Valdovias was measured—a strategic choice, especially if they needed future help. They also respected Esteban Valdovia's job as a rural schoolteacher, which allowed him a monthly salary from the federal government and health care for the family at the more prestigious hospital, the Instituto de Seguridad y Servicios Sociales de los Trabajadores del Estado (ISSTE). Francisca Valdovia had four children and worked at home, at first making clothes to sell in the downtown market. Later, when her children were in school, she had her own stall in the colonia market and would hire other women such as Aída and Gloria to do the sewing for her. As a result of being seen as a boss, Francisca maintained only formal relationships with colonia women and kept to her close friends in the city, whom she said were in a similar social position to her own. She has always had, and still has, ties to her friends and family in her village, to other market vendors who have the same interests as her own, and to the wives of other schoolteachers. This, she felt, was her proper social milieu, one based fundamentally upon a common social class and economic status, and not on the symbolic and social capital that had, in earlier days, characterized neighborhood and compadre networks of residents such as Berta, Margarita, and María.

The Valdovia family affected certain middle-class mannerisms and dispositions. Their attitudes and outlooks can perhaps be explained in two ways. First, over a period of fifteen years, as their living standard improved, their style of living and their demeanor in the colonia changed accordingly. Second, they came from Oaxacan valley mestizo villages where they were not the poorest families, but rather in the middle of the economic strata. This is significant because the income of Esteban's family in the village was enough to allow him to attend lower and upper secondary school (grades 7–12) and to make the move to the city. Given his position in the village, and the calculation that we can presume to have been made to send him to school, one might suggest that his family background fostered the dispositions that helped him make certain economically rationalized choices, which then allowed him to take advantage of the possibilities that the future offered. Thus when the couple moved to Colonia Hermosa, they brought more with them than a steady job. They brought dispositions that supported their upward movement in the class system of the city of Oaxaca.

As with their relationship with Miguel and Gloria, Esteban and Francisca maintained exchange relationships only with those colonia residents who worked in the tequio for the Mesa Directiva—of which they were not only members, but were each president at different times. As a result of the social as well as the economic capital that they possessed, capitals that were recognized by their neighbors, they would always take a patrón position in local affairs, except when interacting with their compadres Enrique Guzmán and his mother. From them, the Valdovia family received symbolic and social capital, which was helpful to establish and maintain their high social standing in the colonia. In return they always offered help and support to Guzmán's family. Such support was not returned, as in this game the Guzmán family took the role of patrón. The fact that Estebán and Francisca did not need the help of family or neighbors to feed and care for their family meant that other colonia residents had nothing but their labor to offer to them. This they took, either by buying the labor, or by using their neighbors when they needed something done. Unlike Guzmán, who was never accused openly, until recently, of using his position in the colonia for personal gain, the Valdovia family was always thought to be conniving, and using their networks in self-interested ways rather than as a help to others. Indeed, some residents felt that every member of the Mesa Directiva was there on behalf of their own interests. These residents were always from the faction who had supported the schoolteacher-turned-developer. They continued to argue that it was only they who had legal title to their land, as they had "purchased" it, as they would say, before Guzmán and his kind arrived on the scene and took over the administration of colonia affairs through their Mesa Directiva.

CONCLUSION

This chapter has focused on the way social capital is formed, used, and rearranged in the colonia community. Social relationships between neighbors and family members are commonly used as key strategies for coping with short-term daily survival and household maintenance. As well, such relationships were used by residents to establish permanent positions within the social field of the colonia hierarchy of social status and prestige. These relationships in the early days of the colonia reveal how the colonia acted as a kind of buffer zone to cushion residents from their daily struggle with poverty. Such strategies for household maintenance were most often part of women's networks, as their roles were so singular in their responsibility for the family's daily health and well-being. Nowadays such community-based relationships have been completely transformed from the community setting and are now focused more narrowly on the expanded natal family.

Colonia residents were initially engaged in high-level and intense communal self-help. The city and governmental structures were completely inadequate to help them to meet their needs. The community worked together to form the infrastructure for basic social services, with little help from the outside. Most women worked for money; they tended to work at home, doing laundry, sewing piecework items for the market, or making food to sell door-to-door in the city. Being at home allowed them to make and to use family ties, neighborly friendships, and comadre ties to secure their daily needs when their own cupboards were bare, and when they needed someone to watch their children. A clear example is afforded by the complex system of neighborhood credit extended to families such as María's and Aída's. Like many colonia residents, they did not, in the past, use banks, because they had little or no surplus money, and because the written contracts and logic of banking were too alien and presented too abstract an idea of the future to have been of practical use. Aside from pawning household items, when a family needed extra money, they did one of two things: they would borrow from a local moneylender at 10 to 15 percent per month, or they would borrow from a patrón or a compadre. In this relationship it was the persona and the personal, the role of symbolic capital that acted as collateral, since the relationship was always assumed to outlast the transaction. The most impoverished families displayed the greatest variation in their strategies and their use of social relationships to meet daily needs because they were on the receiving, or client, end of most relationships, except for those with their friends. They were the first to ask for help, and first to offer labor, as opposed to money or goods, to their compadres in the city.

In contrast to María and Aída, we should remember the Valdovia family. Their use of various social relationships were such that they were able to move upwards in terms of economic worth (from the Mesa Directiva to ownership in the new market), and also in social position and cultural capital, knowledge and education. Such relationships worked within a sense of the future calculated to change class position, even though it may not have been directly and consciously constructed to do so.

As of the year 2000, most of the women in my study, even the older ones, were continuing to work for money. Until shortly before her death, even María continued to have a little soda pop store in her house and sometimes made mole enchiladas to sell. Their adult daughters also work, but less often at home. Many have succeeded in obtaining job training, and this takes them away from home, leaving their children at school or with their grandparents or other family members. The women who now stay at home have either created restaurants in their living rooms to serve the local students, such as Leticia, or others, like Consuelo, will work generally away from home selling products. While their incomes may have grown, their lives have become more complicated by changing work structures in Mexico. These structures have also had an impact on their networks with other women. Generally today women do not go to their compadres for help but rather to their siblings. Even this pattern has changed, however, as we see the impact of economic capital and the ideology of individual achievement act upon even intimate family interactions as the question of status and achievement now take their place in the space of family relationships in a way not seen before.

Consequently, we might ask, what is the place, the position of compadres, in the field of social relations and their resulting connections to social networks and social strategies? In the year 2000 I found that while families were still involved in compadre relationships, such connections were often work-related and not comparable to the support systems of twenty or thirty years earlier. For instance, Alejandro and his wife do have compadres from their wedding, but these were friends made at Alejandro's workplace. As Alejandro has changed work sites, they no longer see one another and are never called upon in times of need. The closest compadre ties are now attached to sibling ties, which means that women and men have a more limited range of serious friendship networks than before. So, while they all maintain that they are part of the city of Oaxaca, in reality their world has shrunk in one sense, because their social ties are more limited—mostly to their adult siblings.

Another element of the changes that have occurred with regard to compadre relations is the lessening of ties to the Catholic Church and the fundamental religious practices that have always been central to traditional compadre relationships. The current residents of Colonia Hermosa may continue to maintain allegiance to Catholicism (should anyone ask them), but most of them do not maintain a close connection to rituals or to a particular local church. In fact, even thirty years ago, the local Catholic church all but ignored colonia residents and never made overtures to any of the residents. Members of the clergy never appeared in the colonia, which was less than one-quarter mile away; they never fostered community-church relationships, and they never offered help to the poor in the colonia. When Consuelo and her first husband, Roberto, wanted to get married in a church ceremony, the priest declined their request on the basis that Consuelo's parents were not properly married in the church and therefore no better than common-law partners—which was a sin and which made their children all illegitimate. Thus their daughter would not have her wedding consecrated.

While the relationship today with the local Catholic Church is similar, there has been one important change in Colonia Hermosa, and that is the rise of Pentecostal and Evangelical Christian activity. In 2000 there were at least four local churches right in the colonia, as well as an evangelical group that was providing clothes and other necessities to the poor. The new evangelical activities are taking place right in the middle of the colonia where once I was not spoken to in case I was a Protestant! As compadre relationships are not part of the Protestant church, it may well be that different religious activities and beliefs will make further changes to these traditional forms of personal relationships.

CHAPTER 7

THE DISENCHANTED WORLD AND
THE QUESTION OF SUCCESS

MY INVESTIGATION INTO THE LIVES of Colonia Hermosa residents asked a classical migration question: "Why do some rural migrants to the city succeed while others, and their children, do not?" I sought to uncover the particular strategies and social logics that could account for the trajectories of the lives of colonia residents over three decades in the city of Oaxaca, Mexico. I have concentrated on a comparative account of the life transitions as experienced by a group of key families with regard to two points: their sense of social place, and their sense of their own identities. I have argued that over the past three decades colonia residents have transformed their class positions through a strategic use of scarce resources, as well as through the use of a variety of symbolic and social capitals.

What are we now to make of the lives of the people who have shared their stories in this book? What conclusions can we draw from their individual and collective narratives that we can use to generally interpret the lives of the urban poor? How might the structural position of the urban poor in any developing capitalist society be helped by lessons learned in Colonia Hermosa? I would argue that across a variety of cultural spaces, people confront common problems in a globalized world. As Colonia Hermosa residents were able to create everyday practices that helped the community function and prosper, perhaps their approach can be used by and expanded upon by others. As June Nash has argued, anthropologists, students, and others working for the common good can help through creating cross-cultural comparative frameworks of analysis that in the end are good for people across the planet.[1]

The jumping-off point for the study was the transformation in self-identity as expressed by my informants, who routinely said that they felt that they had successfully moved from the category of transitory migrant to permanent urban citizen. They live now in a city that they feel is their own. As new migrants, the physical space of a squatter settlement worked in opposition to the established city, and this geographical opposition reflected the powerful social oppositions of class, language, and personal habitus that separated middle- and working-class city dwellers from the squatters. Colonia residents were set apart from others by the social space that they inhabited, the physical spaces that they lived in, and by the way they viewed the world. Many of the residents were initially drawn to Colonia Hermosa through radio and newspaper advertisements offering land sites. Their initial sense of urban identity was thus, in part, structured by a particular time and place in the development of Oaxaca—an important historical dimension, which continued to influence the new inhabitants until they received titles to their land. This reveals to us, as so many other studies have done, the importance of families owning their own homes and, at least, feeling secure in their tenancy in a location, a physical place that is habitable because it has basic services: sewage connections, bottled potable water services, and electricity.

Today, as Colonia Hermosa continues to develop as a suburb of the city, and residents are now considered formally part of the urban citizenry, such oppositions between original holders of land titles and those who were said to be illegal land tenants have faded into the background, while simultaneously others based upon achievement have been revealed. Each and every person I worked with spoke of individual achievement. They all declared to me that their lives over the past thirty years had been successful—despite the challenges they had faced, and the fact that many still work day-to-day to support themselves without employment benefits, and only family help to rely upon in difficult times.

There are two central means by which I feel that we can understand their perspective. One way to view how colonos speak about their lives is as their rationalized accounts of the logic that lies within the structure of capital. A second avenue is the recognition by my informants of their own dignity and grace, derived from a hard-won life. Using the first approach, which involves the language of empire, we can account for their success narratives as being a situation of *méconnaisance*, or misrecognition, deriving from the fact that they all continue to live the hard lives of the working poor. But by claiming success, they use the language of empire to rationalize their lives (as we all must) within the structure of capital.

Using the second approach of analysis, as colonos take credit for their work and their lives, we can recognize their vision of success as reflecting a measure of control over daily life that they have gained through hard work, prayer, and a series of strategies, all of which have allowed them to use and transform whatever capitals they had at hand. Such strategies now give them some sense of economic safety and self-respect. To my mind, both approaches carry the weight of truth.

What this study demonstrates is that the daily practice of colonia residents such as Consuelo, Theresa, and Aída is a logical outcome of the interaction of the larger structures (economics, politics) that limit the field and capitals available to colonos, along with the social and territorial spaces in which they live, plus their personal dispositions, which help to structure particular choices they may take at certain moments, and the use of various capitals that they have invoked. Thus, we can clearly see that the structure of economic and social practices in Colonia Hermosa results from the mutual processes of individual dispositions and the objective structures of urban Oaxacan society. In the years between 1968 and 1974, residents expressed their primary expectations in very concrete terms: to secure a steady job, health care, and primary schooling for their children, as well as job training when their children finished primary school. This was the image of an anticipated future that they carried with them as they migrated to the city of Oaxaca and began their lives in Colonia Hermosa. This is what constituted a successful life for their imagined futures.

In the year 2000, colonos' views were unchanged. In both time frames, there was an underlying paradigm that not only connects the two disparate time periods, but also reveals a common interpretation, a shared social habitus, of what a successful life means to them: hard work, religious practice and an adherence to God's grace and favor, mutual help within families, and the benefits of training that would ensure job security—which is, for them, the bottom line. What this commonality implies to me is that there exists within the larger discourse a taken-for-granted understanding, or a doxic structure, implicit in community life. This doxic understanding was the foundation for their initial move to the colonia, it was foundational to the work of the Mesa Directiva, and it was what propelled at least some of the children in each family to finish primary school and complete job training courses. I would argue that this logic underlies the generational transformation of squatters as they become acclimated to the developing capitalist urban world.

The goals that colonia residents and, in general, the urban poor aspire to are not a series of human rights. Given the structure of state and globalized capital in which they live, this largest group of humanity understands perfectly well that there are few human rights available to them by the state. Rather, at least from the view of Colonia Hermosa residents, they view their lives and rights as direct products of their personal struggles: struggles to build a place and to fashion a future for themselves and their families. In these struggles, born from the indignity of social injustice, they also make clear to the world, through their narrative histories, their personal and collective dignity. This does not mean, however, that they have any illusions about the justice of the social structure. Time and time again, colonos have criticized their state and national governments for not helping other poor people, primarily by not creating jobs. The government, they say, should help others so that no one has to suffer as they did.

In the first stages of Colonia Hermosa settlement, social capital was widely used. In order to secure basic services and titles to their land, residents came together through the Mesa Directiva in the tequio, which functioned to give the colonia an identity and which worked to provide initial services of electricity and water and to build a school. The Mesa also built the first dirt roads and paths, and dug the first water holes for the families in the upper sections of the colonia. Although the first phase of colonia development began with an argument between factions and a court case, nowadays this argument, as well as the communal work that first defined the colonia, is dismissed as a relic and is no longer considered important. There has been a parallel movement between people's accumulation of personal and family resources as opposed to communal and neighborly help, and the move of the colonia from being an extra-legal settlement to a legitimate city suburb. As a result, the success of community work and networks has faded into the background and no longer figures in people's accounts of their lives. What this means also is that the social field of the colonia has not only changed in nature and quality, but is no longer considered the anchor that it once was for family and community identity. Today the major fields of social practice lay within the family, in the field of work, in commodity production and consumption, and for some, the field of educational achievement.

Residents' success in obtaining titles to their land and houses was born of their collective work. To my mind, this was the central, critical step that helped transform their lives in the city. As is clear from

Chapter 4, gaining legal titles has allowed them to be free of monthly mortgage or rent payments. It provided a security of tenure, and a place for their grown children to continue to live and build their own homes. Security of tenure allowed residents to focus economic support, time, and attention on the nuclear family. Children and their spouses care for parents, as well as contribute to the maintenance and development of the home compound. Without this level of basic security, it is questionable as to whether any of the children of my initial informants would have been able to complete any schooling or secure employment. Even with guaranteed housing, some children (such as Consuelo, Leticia, Moises, Alejandro, and Gustavo) neither completed their education nor found stable employment with benefits. How much more improbable would it have been for other siblings to become nurses or engineers without the security of their parents' home, however humble?

A second benefit that accrued from both the collective labor of the tequio and government help is the creation of a local school in Colonia Hermosa, even if some children did not attend regularly. Forming the school was part of the work of the Mesa Directiva and colonia residents, who so firmly believed in the benefits of education that they began building the first primary school classroom. As well, we must not forget the lobbying efforts that the same leaders made to the local and state governments for the school, and how these government bodies responded (during election years) in a positive way. In this fashion, the school was constructed through the joint use of the people's labor and government materials. The benefits of being able to send one's child down the road to school are obviously very great; however, given the economic structures that most colonia families lived in, the school itself was not an unambiguous good. I remember that each Monday the teachers would have all the students march around the playground to the tunes of nationalistic songs. Students were also required to wear white shirts and trousers or skirts that day. Many of my informants' children did not own such clothes, so they regularly missed school. As well, many girls stayed at home, helping their mothers, while their brothers often went along to work with their fathers if they were construction workers in the city. Sometimes they left school at midday to bring their fathers the lunch that their mothers had made. When children did attend school, they often lacked the simple tools of pencils, paper, and books, which families were expected to subsidize. Thus even early schooling was not the clearly defined, seamless path of six years of study, as some would have us believe. Many residents, such as

Consuelo and Leticia, did not finish primary school until age fourteen. The same situation still exists for other poor children in Oaxaca, the new migrants to the colonia who live far up on the hillside.

As the employment trajectories of colonia residents demonstrate, a large part of their social suffering and continued poverty is a reflection of their relationship to the educational system, which did little to help them succeed. Their lack of educational cultural capital shaped whatever social or economic capitals they could accrue, and, as well, the way they have imagined their futures—as circumscribed by their family and class habitus. That being said, everyone in Colonia Hermosa now *claims* to have a primary school certificate (except for the very elderly), and this has helped individuals find work. In fact, by the year 2000, some employers required workers to provide a primary school certificate as proof of attendance and graduation.

As discussed in Chapter 5, beginning in the late 1970s there was an expansion of local educational opportunities with the upgrading of technical and professional schools. Thus, women such as Marisol and Alicia (Santiago's wife) were able to train as nurses in the local technical college, which also trained some colonia adolescents to perform regional dances.[2] After this training, students could choose to work as government employees who traveled to schools and local villages to dance in fiestas, thereby keeping some of the traditional music and dances alive. They also often work at tourist hotels. Such skills are marketable in Oaxaca, where tourists search for so-called authentic traditional performances. In fact this is what Moises did, and during one of his performances he met his wife-to-be and her father, who later taught him the business of carving and painting wooden animals for the tourist trade.

Job opportunities, job security, and health benefits have always been central concerns for Colonia Hermosa residents. For some, these goals were a major component of their own lives and those of their children. When I first lived in the colonia, residents felt that the government (however they defined it) was responsible for building industry in Oaxaca so that people could find work, even though they did not have faith that this would ever happen. When I returned in the late 1990s, they still felt that it was the responsibility of government to encourage industry and to help new migrants find jobs. In this way, colonia residents were still sensitive to the terrible hardships that new migrants go through to sustain themselves, and, similarly, they acknowledge their kinship with newcomers through the knowledge of poverty, which they all suffered from at one time or another. So, while colonia families do argue that one's future livelihood depends on hard work, prayer, and strategic choices, they do not argue that others must suffer in the same way. They do not take the arrogant position that others should "pull themselves up by their bootstraps," except (and this is an important exception) those individuals who are judged to be unworthy of help or sympathy because of their own failings, such as being lazy, drinking to excess, or living a dissolute life.

Within the sentiments of colonia residents that government should help the poor find work, and in their history of helping their neighbors and family members, we perhaps glimpse an example of Zygmunt Bauman's thesis at work: that being moral, though not defined as being good, is the constitutive attribute of humanity, and one which makes "the human condition unique and sets it apart from any other modes of being-in-the-world" (Bauman and Tester 2001: 44). It is through their empathy for others and their common sense about the world that colonos remind us how to live together in the world of globalized capital and power structures. I feel that this is their challenge to us, though, I would argue, not one that they are conscious of.

In Chapter 5 I reviewed the jobs of Colonia Hermosa residents. Most of them are self-employed, without benefits or real security, save the security of their own energy and actions. Today, as the city has grown, and as the tourist industry has become more central to the city's economic life, increasing numbers of colonia residents have found jobs in service industries, such as delivering bottled water, working in hotels, and creating items from popular culture to tourists. While employment has increased in Oaxaca, there has been a parallel increase in both the formal and informal occupational sectors, which means that the distinction between the very poor and the minimum-wage earner is now more marked. For instance, work opportunities for those without a steady job continue to be scarce (as in the lives of Consuelo, Alejandro, and Gustavo). Their lives are constrained by having to move from one small project to another. A worker may be abandoned once a project is over. As with all urban poor citizens, being employed is not taken for granted, and they fall back on old subsistence patterns even as they claim to be involved in new ideas and new types of jobs. For instance, Consuelo's door-to-door sales and her trips to the coast and her sister Leticia's food sales from her home both mimic their mother's work history. But they do not see this correspondence. Or, consider the contract labor jobs that Alejandro takes, or his work trips to the United

States, which are now viewed as regular and are, for so many of the poor, a viable alternative as they search for work and income. This is still contract labor, akin to that offered to the men who stood on the street corners in downtown Oaxaca, but who are now in downtown Los Angeles.

Even government work contracts do not guarantee secure employment. Although some colonia residents, such as Consuelo's father, Alfredo, were able to benefit from a new federal contract, their work was still dependent on an informal agreement between laborers and the independent contractor, and was not secured by union contract or written agreement. Even when the federal government is paying the workers directly, job security is not always part of the mutual understanding.

It is clear from these accounts that as each family continued to survive and build its support system through their children year by year, and as Colonia Hermosa became a legitimate, designated suburb of Oaxaca, personal and community identities changed from that of migrants to established urban citizens. As is clear from Chapter 6, women and their neighborly support networks and compadre relationships were critical for their mutual survival in the early days of the colonia. Today, support networks are generally restricted to the family, and do not include neighbors or compadres, as grown children help to support their parents and, in some ways, extend help to their siblings, though never as generously as they do towards their parents. What is interesting is that those who are most reliant on family help do not recognize it as being a critical part of their ability to survive. The move from neighborly help to a more individual focus is expressed in the way that residents reflect a much more confident attitude in their business dealings with local city structures and with institutions such as banks. In a Bourdieuian sense, many colonia residents have learned to play the game of the city—but not everyone.

Many transformations are taking place in the emergent Mexican society. Even though each of my informants claimed success, only half of the generation of children who are now adults can be said to have escaped from extreme poverty into the comparative safety of the working class, and even fewer into the middle class. Many still live in desperate poverty and work in highly exploitative situations, although in some cases their siblings have fared better. Still, they see themselves as moving in an upward trajectory. The explanation for the discontinuity between perceptions and daily struggles must be found in the space of ideology, an ideology that tells them that they are succeeding because they do work hard, and because they have been able to acquire certain material resources, such as furniture, or a refrigerator, or even an old and unreliable car. In Chapter 3, I suggested that among those whose lives are characterized by unstable employment, no health care, and little entitlement, many fail to recognize the actual truth of their situation when they claim success. From a theoretical level, we can argue that *méconnaisance* makes survival possible for all of us, and allows life to go on, because such is the logic of late capital and the needs of the marketplace. By this I mean that misunderstandings of the reality of objective structures are often what makes existence bearable. Facing up to whatever passes for the truth minute by minute would, for most of us, be unbearable and prevent constructive action.

Colonos now argue that if one is to thrive in the city, one must focus upon individual achievement, and the communal aspect of life—getting land titles, connecting water lines, and building the school—has faded into the background. While individual success was always part of their picture of urban life in the colonia, a sense of community was never so lacking as it is now. In this way, we can understand how dispositions from family and community transform historically and begin to be situated more deeply in the overarching ideology of the market economy.

In reading the stories of Colonia Hermosa residents, we are reminded that people are not beings that move only when they react to external situations, but rather are agents who create possibilities and lives for themselves. As Gramsci (1991) (and Marx) long ago argued, men and women are possessed of the ability and the power to make the world for themselves—though they are often hindered by the prevailing ordering structures. By squatting on land, building their own homes, and getting basic amenities for their community, one could argue that at the beginning of their residence in Oaxaca, my informants acted in unauthorized ways. At the same time they worked within a paradigm of common sense, closely connected to the views of the prevailing government and social structures, as they never believed their futures to be in anyone's hands but their own, for good or for ill. As well, even as the national Mexican government abdicated its responsibility for its poor, it benefited from the work of squatters as they built their own community infrastructures.

Finally, on the basis of the personal and community narratives shared in this book, we have an opportunity to explore how the individuals in Colonia Hermosa are connected to our own lives, and whether they might be able to shed light on life for us all, within a world increasingly driven by the larger collective machine of globalized capital. We also might consider if this phenomenon brings us closer together in some way. In recognizing our common predicament and our common humanity, we can begin, as Bauman suggests, to reconstitute society as the common property and common responsibility of free individuals aiming at a dignified life (Bauman and Tester 2001: 106).

CLOSING REMARKS

There are two major connections that I have chosen to discuss briefly here, and which serve to end the book: consumerism and the globalization of employment. Our lives are connected to those of the residents of Colonia Hermosa through the positive and negative benefits of living in a consumer society. My informants are extremely proud of their reestablished homes, complete with refrigerators, beds, televisions, and proper sewage and (nonpotable) water connections. Recall from Chapter 4 how each family took me through their homes, each one having been rebuilt or modernized, and each filled with a variety of objects and consumer items. This, for them, was material proof of their hard work, of how far they had come from having one bed for eight family members and using boxes to hold their belongings. This new, more consumer-oriented life reflected, for them, the dignity of their existence, and also their transformation from poor migrants to urban citizens. For them, their houses and consumer objects were proof that they had been successful at playing the game. This is, in part, because the poor (and the middle class) live in a world that is dominated by the material standards of the rich.

Along with those standards goes an implicit moral standard that characterizes those who are not successful in this material way as flawed and good for nothing (Bauman and Tester 2001; Wacquant 1999). I also heard this same evaluation from my informants as they accounted for family members or friends whom they did not consider to be successful. In short, they would make the claim that such individuals were thought to be lazy or lacking in any strategic sense. As they said over and over, "the opportunities are out there. One must simply take advantage of them." As increasing numbers of individuals offer this accepted explanation for individual and family failures in the economic and social fields (including, and perhaps especially, in the developed world), people are increasingly, as Canclini (1993: 64) argues, "individuals without a community, seekers of a solitary place in a system that evades [us]." The consequence, for many, is that while we are more connected through commerce, travel, and even the Internet, we are more solitary in the search for our lives within developing capital. This serves to weaken community bonds and creates huge obstacles to social justice. In the United States we are masters of the consumer society and the individuation—the separation from the social—that consumer society demands. Some have argued that the rise of the skillful consumer is the fall of the citizen, which implies people no longer take responsibility for the society in which they live (Bauman and Tester 2001: 114). So, what we in Mexico and in the United States might ask ourselves is the following: Is this the kind of society that we want? Is this the kind of society that is actually sustainable? Will such a society successfully provide us with what we need at the deepest levels? The lives of Colonia Hermosa residents and the lessons that their stories teach us require us to consider such questions for our common future.

A second particular connection that exists between ourselves and the lives of my informants rests within the field of employment. We are all connected through networks of global capital, and this connection has an enormous impact on all of our working lives. In the developing world, job security has always been tenuous for the poor. Now, given the connections between large corporations, international markets, and blue- and white-collar workers, job insecurity is everywhere: in the private sector as well in as the public sector, which is increasing the number of temporary or part-time positions. What this contributes towards—for us all, but especially the unemployed—is what Bourdieu calls the casualization of labor, which makes "the whole future uncertain [and] prevents all rational anticipation. . . ." (Bourdieu 1998: 82). The personal and collective insecurity produced by job instability is a growing form of symbolic violence and domination by states and corporations.

This situation does not, however, preclude struggle against such a system. So, while Bourdieu's comment gives us grounds for worry, we should not disregard the power—as exemplified through the lives of my informants—of self-determination as created through community and family bonds. Instead, we can take heart from their example and understand that creating a society based on social justice will require our individual and collective commitment—not with great fanfare, but in our ordinary, daily practice. As Bourdieu reminds us, "nothing is less innocent than noninterference" (Bourdieu et al. 2000: 629).

CHAPTER SUMMARIES AND DISCUSSION
QUESTIONS FOR TEACHERS AND STUDENTS

INTRODUCTION

IN THE INTRODUCTION I discuss the book and its main topic, which is the Colonia Hermosa and its residents, by beginning with the term *disenchantment*, the change from what was a "natural" world of sociability to one that has been reduced to its economic dimension. I argue that one can understand the transformation from migrant to urban citizen through a process of disenchantment, a concept that is linked to the work of both Max Weber and Pierre Bourdieu. I also discuss the importance of positionality with regard to fieldwork and the need for anthropologists to be reflexive in their practice. By this account, I hope that the reader will understand that though the social scientist conducts interviews, records life histories, and even takes surveys, we all see the world through the lens of our personal and class habitus. As a result we must acknowledge the weight of our own histories on the work we produce. As an example, I give a brief overview of my initial approach to working in Colonia Hermosa.

In the classroom the introduction may form as the basis for a series of "free-writes" or class discussions on the following topics:

1. Students may consider their own work in the light of their own positionality. What do you bring to the table? What do you carry as you begin a project?
2. Do you understand the term *disenchantment*? How might you imagine the term to be useful?
3. How do you think or imagine that people change class positions in society? Perhaps you have the experiences of your own families to

reflect upon. You might also consider how you view society as being connected to the individual.

CHAPTER 1

In this chapter I begin with a description of the birth of a child by my informant, Gloria Sánchez. The birth took place in a private clinic operated specifically for his poorer patients by a local Oaxacan doctor. He also operates a clinic for his wealthy clients where the service is much better. I use the example so that readers will think about the notion of symbolic violence as it pervades the most intimate aspects of the lives of the poor. The challenges faced by the Sánchez family are no different than those faced by most urban poor migrants. In the following sections of the chapter I discuss the state of Oaxaca in general and Colonia Hermosa in detail, and why it is that people migrate to the city—a common phenomenon all over the world. The goal is to have readers appreciate the larger view of migration as it is situated in a specific time and place.

In the classroom I would suggest that students focus on the following suggested topics for their discussions and free-writes:

1. What is meant by the term "symbolic violence"? Can you understand this as existing in a person's everyday life?
2. Discuss the challenges of migration for those who migrate and the cities and towns that receive migrants.
3. Identify the key elements that helped Colonia Hermosa to become a successful community as well as a city suburb. What level of interaction between residents was necessary in order for this to happen?

CHAPTER 2

In this chapter I particularly focus on the reflexive nature of the construction of research projects as I discuss the central problem that structures this book. The three central players in the process were the residents from Colonia Hermosa, myself, and the larger field of migrant studies in Latin America. A second central issue discussed in the chapter is how both the personal and the structural combine to create everyday, practical lives. Thus, I discuss the analytical structure put forward by Pierre Bourdieu, which I use in the book.

In the classroom, students might discuss or write about Bourdieu's method in the context of the following topics:

1. How does social science help to construct what the investigator "sees"? Why is this important?
2. Give a real-life example of how habitus, field, and different types of capital work together in our daily social practice.

CHAPTER 3

In this chapter readers have an opportunity to become acquainted with one particular woman, Consuelo. Her life has been used as an example of the lives of women in the colonia in particular, and among the Oaxacan urban poor in general. The challenges she faces and the personal choices she has made over the past thirty years reflect not only the personal circumstances of her life, but also the many changes that have occurred in Colonia Hermosa and the city of Oaxaca. Through this rather detailed life history, readers should be able to comprehend how habitus and the larger objective structures of society have helped to create Consuelo's actual day-to-day life.

In the classroom, students could discuss the strategies that Consuelo has chosen in order to have what she considers to be a successful life. Why are such strategies reflective of her class position, her upbringing, and her own dispositions? I would also suggest that students consider the question of *méconnaisance* as it is discussed in the conclusion of the chapter. This term does *not* imply self-delusion, but a misunderstanding and misapprehension of objective structures—those which, in part, structure and constrain lives in society. Such structures are themselves authorized by society. Being so, "the real dimensions of the social order" are misrecognized, and misrecognition "contributes to the reproduction of that order" (Bourdieu 1972: 163).

CHAPTER 4

This chapter focuses on Colonia Hermosa settlement stories, and how house sites and identities have changed over the past thirty years. I begin the chapter with my own arrival in Colonia Hermosa with my university adviser and other graduate students. One important point that each narrative has in common is that residents feel that their material acquisitions are symbolic of their successes in the city, and also reflect the struggles for survival and basic existence that have engaged them over the years. Moreover, house sites themselves have become a spatial metaphor of their successes and their future aspirations. The chapter takes detailed notice of the lives of three households that are representative of colonia residents: a mother-centered household, a family of indigenous migrants (the husband and wife speaking two different indigenous languages as their first language), and a Mestizo household in which the husband is from Oaxaca city, and the wife is from the coast of Oaxaca.

I would suggest that students discuss in the classroom or write about the impact that communal work had on the construction of Colonia Hermosa. I also suggest a discussion about how families are now focused more closely on individual projects as opposed to community projects. It is important here that readers appreciate the changes and choices that the members of each family made as their lives were transformed over the past thirty years. I think also that readers will appreciate that not everyone has changed class position in those years. I suggest discussion questions on such topics.

CHAPTER 5

The focus of Chapter 5 is work: how work structures the lives of Colonia Hermosa residents, and how it impacts their sense of self-identity. Again, the theoretical apparatuses used are the familiar habitus and personal agency, field and capitals, and the concept of human lives as a product of the interaction of all three. In the first example, the life of Alejandro, I discuss how both structure and agency are at work in the unfolding of his life, especially as they are connected to his work history. The chapter also brings together data from structured interviews with colonia residents that reveal not only the occupational structure of the colonia in the early 1970s, but also the types of capital that were valued at that time in their social hierarchy. One important point that readers and students might consider is the use of money and strategies of economic behavior that might work against successfully "playing the game" in the urban economy, but which, because of the focus on symbolic and cultural capitals, are critical in their ability to create a more enjoyable life.

For student discussions and free-writes, I suggest topics related to the following:

1. School and work
2. Social reproduction of class and family habitus
3. How economic success for some has created a gap between family members and colonia families

CHAPTER 6

Chapter 6 discusses the use of social relationships between women, families, and compadres and how they function as social capital, which in the past served as a safety net for family survival. These early relationships served as a support system along with the larger support system of colonia communal projects that helped residents with electricity, water, and title issues. Nowadays, support is no longer rooted in one's neighbors or compadres but within the extended family of siblings and their parents. Even when not acknowledged by those who benefit from the support of their siblings, individuals such as Consuelo rely upon the use of this strategy. The chapter revolves around the stories of two single mothers who are among those defined as "poor" in the colonia, four women in conventional relationships and whose economic and social status was defined as being "regular," and three families considered "wealthy." In the end we see how community-based relationships have completely transformed.

In the classroom, students might write about these families and how each one has chose a particular strategy by which they not only survived, but in some cases were extremely successful in their social as well as in their economic lives. I also suggest that students discuss how the economic and the social combine to reproduce wealth and other types of capital. The point here is to understand how capitals are transformable and how family capital (economic, social, and symbolic) can serve to ensure children's futures—though not in any seamless manner.

CHAPTER 7

There are two central concerns in this chapter. The first is the compelling certainty that residents of Colonia Hermosa have regarding their accomplishments and their sense of success. Strength of character resonates throughout their stories. The second concern is the connection between their lives and ours: I argue that we are all connected in a very material way through the web of global capitalism in terms of our consumer behavior and the fact that global employment structures and large corporations now impact all of our lives.

A central question that I would have students discuss and write about is whether or not social injustice was an important factor in shaping the lives of Colonia Hermosa residents. I would also suggest that students consider how to define social justice, given that we all come into the world with different competencies and personalities, and grow up with our own family and personal dispositions. How might it be possible to allow for our differences and yet offer as near a level playing field as possible? And, is this a good thing?

Finally, given the economic difficulties associated with the recent global recession, students may benefit from writing how they and their families are connected, not personally, but to the people and economy of Mexico. This is a very large question. Therefore, students could work in groups to establish the boundaries of the discussion as well as the ethnographic data to investigate the problem.

INTRODUCTION

1. See Jim Wallis, *God's Politics: Why The Right Gets It Wrong and the Left Doesn't Get It* (2006).

2. See, among others, the recent *New York Times* article by Louis Uchitelle, "Age of Riches: The Richest of the Rich, Proud of a New Gilded Age," (July 15, 2007).

3. In the *New York Times* article cited above, note the self-congratulatory tone of, for example, Sanford Weill, late chairman of Citigroup, who has his office lined with portraits of himself from the various instruments of the media.

4. See Max Weber, "Science as a Vocation," a lecture first given in 1918 in Munich and republished in many places, including *The Vocation Lectures* (2004).

5. See Scott Cook, *Understanding Commodity Cultures: Explorations in Economic Anthropology with Case Studies from Mexico* (2004).

6. See Charles Golden, "Where Does Memory Reside, and Why Isn't It History?" (2005).

7. See Charles Valentine, *Culture and Poverty* (1968).

8. I had not yet realized at that time that the state is actually an ambiguous reality—though never neutral—existing as a set of institutions and, as well, existing in the minds of its polity.

9. A tequio is a community-based work group with roots in traditional village society.

10. By "global capitalism" I do not refer to a homogenous marketplace, but to the hold of a small number of dominant nations over the whole of national financial markets, which then, as a consequence, comes to redefine the international division of labor (Bourdieu 1998: 38).

ONE

1. Susto is a traditional folk illness commonly defined as fright. See Arthur Rubel et al., *Susto: A Folk Illness* (1991).

2. Personal communication from Prof. V. M. Rodriguez.

3. See selections from the prison notebooks of Antonio Gramsci (1991).

4. See in particular John Chance 1977, 1978 and John Paddock 1966.

5. The experience of family members in the military and in the new bureaucracies and tourist industries is communicated back to those who still labor in the countryside.

6. Oaxaca is characterized by Mexican census material as being very poor in comparison to other, more northerly states in Mexico. Oaxaqueños also think of themselves and their state as being poor. In the late 1960s and 1970s, colonia residents felt that the general reason for this poverty was the lack of industrialization, which would employ much of the population, as well as the lack of effective transportation. At that time, the highway system that linked Oaxaca with Mexico City

wound its way through the mountainous regions and was extremely slow and difficult to drive.

7. The Trique language is part of the Mixtecan language family.

8. Regarding legal squatters' rights, Mexican law confers possession rights on
people who have occupied a plot for ten or more years. In the city of Oaxaca this
constitutes approximately 15 percent of the households. Another 26 percent occupy
land to which they do not hold any recognizable title, but of which they consider
themselves the owners, and which they effectively control. With the hope of pro-
moting further private urban housing development, the National Commission for
the Regularization of Land Tenure (CORETT) was established. For a fee, they confer
legal title on a lot's current residents. But as soon as they are registered, they are
vulnerable to government taxes, making for an uneasy alliance of squatters and government (Murphy and Stepick 1991: 66).

9. The story of colonia land as a social and political relationship has already
been explored more fully in Mahar 2000.

TWO

1. "Habitus" is Bourdieu's term for the "durable dispositions" that shape and
frame behaviors, and social practice in general, for individuals, families, and social
classes.

2. I realize that there is some controversy in the use of these terms.

3. See the most recent work in psychobiography of Dr. William Todd Schultz in
Handbook of Psychobiography (2005).

4. See Richard Harker, Cheleen Mahar, and Christopher Wilkes (eds.), *The Practice of Theory: An Introduction to the Work of Pierre Bourdieu* (1990); Cheleen Mahar,
"An Exercise in Practice: Studying Migrants in Latin American Squatter Settlements"
(1992).

5. The data collected examines household economic practices and draws extensively on ethnographic research completed during 1968–1974, written interviews
with key informants from 1979 to 1982, and interviews with the same informants
and their children from 1996 to 1999.

THREE

1. Consuelo did have an older sister who married into a village family at age
fifteen and, as mentioned above, died in childbirth at sixteen. Her older brother
also worked for the family for two years as a helper on a second-class bus. He died
from injuries sustained as the bus plunged down a ravine on its way to the coast of
Oaxaca.

2. This corresponds to completing grades 1–8 in the United States, or primary
school and 1st–2nd forms in the United Kingdom.

3. Like her mother, Consuelo's small business ventures sometimes lose money.
Her mother would often spend much more money on making food for sale than she
ever brought back. Thus the work was not for economic gain (though misrecognized
as such) but rather offered a way of getting out of the house, and of serving special
food to her family (the leftovers). Consuelo acknowledges the financial problems of

her business, and augments this work with other sales work (clothes and pharmaceuticals) on the coast. Since Consuelo is chronically and heavily in debt, and others in the colonia are not, we can assume that this is one aspect of her life that is quite individual and does not characterize the colonia at large.

4. At that time, "high school" in Oaxaca corresponded to junior high in the United States.

5. Such positions as country doctor and village lawyer fall at the lower end of the middle class in Mexico. While they have none of the security and income that we would associate with parallel professions in first world countries, they do not face continual uncertainty, and although their incomes are modest, they offer a level of security previously unknown in the colonia.

6. The brother who makes and paints wooden animals for the tourist trade has not been successful in his own work and is very dependent on his father-in-law. He is hoping to move into his mother's house in the colonia and to pursue a new line of business. Unlike his brothers, he was trained only in regional dancing, and not for a trade or profession.

FOUR

1. A comadre is a godmother designated through a Catholic ritual, ranging from the very formal ritual of baptism to an informal ritual such as saying a rosary together in church. The relationship that is most important is between the adults because it provides the basis of mutual support. This idea is explored further in Chapter 6.

2. Woven reed mats.

3. An "affinal" relationship is one established through marriage.

4. These are traditional Precolumbian and Mexican cooking implements. The mano and metate are traditional grinding stones, and a comal is a slightly concave griddle, traditionally made of pottery.

5. The tequio is a collective work group of the colonia.

6. Aída was raised by her mother and grandmother. Her father was never spoken of, nor was her grandfather.

7. What is one to make of this discrepancy? As Aída knew very well, by 1979 my own marital history included a divorce. However, I felt as though she continued to "gloss" over her first free union marriage, and for reasons I can only explain as respect for her privacy, I did not press her on this issue, feeling that I was trespassing on her feelings to simply gratify an ethnographer's desire for accuracy on a small point.

8. Aída died in 2007.

9. The Zapotec and Mazatec are indigenous groups in Oaxaca.

10. Inheritance of land in these settings follows a patrilineal pattern, going to sons whose wives often live in the husband's father's compound.

11. The compadrazgo relationship is one founded in Catholicism and literally means "co-parenthood." However, as explained earlier, this relationship is much more a basis of mutual support between the adults involved rather than an actual co-parenting of a child.

12. One interesting item that they had was a refrigerator. As there was no electricity, the refrigerator was used for storage. At one time it held a pile of newspapers.

Later, when I returned in the late 1990s to their new house, I found a refrigerator and gas stove in the cook shack/kitchen. They then saved their newspapers in the oven, because the oven itself did not work.

13. "Indio" is an unfortunate racial epithet that is still used today, often to refer to the indigenous Trique residents who continue to carve their home sites out of the upper reaches of the hillside. Even the chief medical doctor of the Centro de Salud typified poor patients as being "ignorant Indians who wouldn't help themselves."

14. See Chapter 2. He was Consuelo's brother.

15. María died in 1999. In 2000 I visited her grave with Consuelo.

16. Mole is a sauce made from a variety of chilies. There are seven types of mole that are said to have their origins in Oaxaca. In fact, one local restaurant offers a special mole for each day of the week. Mole poblano is made from, among other ingredients, a variety of chiles, ground seeds and nuts, and unsweetened chocolate.

17. The molino is the neighborhood mill for grinding corn into masa.

18. Aída moved to Colonia Hermosa in 1965, and then to her new residence in a new neighborhood in 1985.

19. Posadas are a nine-day Christmas celebration.

20. By 1974 residents of Colonia Hermosa were arguing against having large families. Although most of my informants at that time had more than four children, both women and men said that having children in the city was expensive, and that the families of their own children should be limited to no more than three or four. Even two was acceptable. At that time there was an office of Planned Parenthood in Oaxaca that was funded through the Ford Foundation. The usual clients were not from the city, however, but from the rural areas of Oaxaca (Mahar 1987).

21. I was later to learn that "the factory" consisted of two large freezers for their homemade popsicles.

FIVE

1. Secondary school in Oaxaca is equivalent to middle school plus high school in the United States and United Kingdom: lower secondary school (grades 7–9) and higher secondary school (grades 10–12). Higher secondary school is quite varied. Students may receive three years of preparatory schooling for university work or technological or career job training. Most colonos completed only grades 1–6. If they did attend high school, they have only attended lower high school. More fortunate colonos, such as Consuelo's sister Marisol, attended lower high school and then a nursing job training program. Marisol did not complete university-level nursing studies.

2. See M. Higgins, *Somos gente humilde: Etnografía de una colonia urbana pobre de Oaxaca, Mexico* (1974), and C. Mahar, "From Rural Migrant to Urban Citizen" (2000).

3. All amounts are in U.S. dollars, 1972. Also, all but the professional workers were paid weekly or even daily. These numbers reflect residents' calculations for their general monthly wage.

4. Murphy and Stepick 1991: 96.

5. By 1999 three of these "lending" families that I know were among the wealthiest families in Colonia Hermosa.

6. See M. J. Higgins, "Somos gente humilde," unpublished manuscript, University of Illinois, 1972.

7. At this time most poor families did not have electricity, but hooked up informally to the nearest utility pole.

8. See also Higgins, "Somos gente humilde."

9. See Bourdieu 1990a.

10. See Bourdieu 1990a: 78–80.

SIX

1. These coal stoves, called *anafres*, are a type of brazier. Characteristically, they are made of a thin sheet of metal as a base and shaped into a square about five inches tall. Around the sides of this are four other sheets of thin metal that form a kind of collar that sits on top of the square. Coal is put in the middle of the square, and pots can sit over the coals braced by the collar that is not flat, but tilted upwards.

2. Margarita is married to a first-class truck driver who has a regular route to Mexico City. He used to give her 300 pesos a week to maintain the household. With that allotment, she was expected to purchase all the household needs, make the time payments on some personal items, such as jewelry, and provide their ten children with spending money and school money. It was the husband's responsibility to pay the electric and water bills and to pay for the children's clothing. Their medical costs were covered by government health insurance. Although Margarita received a larger allotment than most women in the colonia, she still had to depend on credit to cover her weekly purchases. She was generally three to four days behind in her credit payments. By the time she got her weekly allotment, she already had bought about three days' worth of goods on credit. In some cases over half of her allotment was used to pay past debts. Many women in the colonia envied Margarita for the money that she received for the household, but an analysis of her buying patterns suggests that the envy was misplaced. Her purchasing patterns were totally within the norm of the colonia: she shopped daily, buying the items around each meal of the day depending on credit. She was able to provide more protein for her family, such as milk, eggs, and meat, but she also had to feed ten children. Margarita did not share the opinion that she was better off than others in the colonia because she was completely dependent upon an often-absent husband.

3. See Chapter 4.

4. At this time, women in Colonia Hermosa generally worked at home most of the time. Even if they were doing laundry for a family in town or selling food on the street or door-to-door, the basic work was always based in the home.

5. CONASUPO was a national cooperative store (National Company of Popular Subsistence) that was not successful in Colonia Hermosa, possibly because foodstuffs were sold there in bulk. Most colonia families were accustomed to buying food daily for reasons of economy and lack of proper storage facilities.

SEVEN

1. See June C. Nash, *Practicing Ethnography in a Globalizing World* (2007).

2. Moises completed this program, as did his sisters Marisol and Aurelia.

Adler Lomnitz, Larissa. 1977. *Networks and Marginality: Life in a Mexican Shanty-town.* New York: Academic Press.

Bauman, Zygmunt, and Keith Tester. 2001. *Conversations with Zygmunt Bauman.* Cambridge: Polity Press.

Bourdieu, Pierre. 1972. *Outline of a Theory of Practice.* Cambridge: Cambridge University Press.

———. 1979a. *Algeria 1960.* Cambridge: Cambridge University Press.

———. 1979b [1984]. *Distinction.* Boston: Harvard University Press.

———. 1990a. *Language and Symbolic Power.* Cambridge, Mass.: Harvard University Press.

———. 1990b. *The Logic of Practice.* Cambridge: Polity Press.

———. 1998. *Acts of Resistance: Against the Tyranny of the Market.* Cambridge: Polity Press.

Bourdieu, Pierre, et al. 2000. *The Weight of the World.* Stanford, Calif.: Stanford University Press.

Brown, J. C. 1972. *Patterns of Intra-Urban Settlement in Mexico City: An Examination of the Turner Theory.* Latin American Studies Program Dissertation Series, no. 40. Ithaca, N.Y.: Cornell University.

Butterworth, Douglas. 1973. "Squatters or Suburbanites? The Growth of Shantytowns in Oaxaca, Mexico." In *Latin American Modernization Problems,* ed. R. E. Scott, 208–32. Urbana: University of Illinois Press.

Butterworth, Douglas, and John Chance. 1981. *Latin American Urbanization.* Cambridge: Cambridge University Press.

Canclini, Nestor Garcia. 1993. *Transforming Modernity: Popular Culture in Mexico.* Austin: University of Texas Press.

———. 1995. *Hybrid Cultures: Strategies of Entering and Leaving Modernity.* Minneapolis: University of Minnesota Press.

Chance, John. 1978. *Race and Class in Colonial Oaxaca.* Palo Alto, Calif.: Stanford University Press.

——— (with W. B. Taylor). 1977. "Estate and Class in a Colonial City: Oaxaca in 1792." In *Comparative Studies in Society and History,* Vol. 19, No. 4 (Oct. 1977): 454–87.

Cohen, Jeffrey H. 1998. "Craft Production and the Challenge of the Global Market: An Artisan's Cooperative in Oaxaca, Mexico." In *Human Organization* (Spring 1998).

Cook, Scott. 2004. *Understanding Commodity Cultures: Explorations in Economic Anthropology with Case Studies from Mexico.* New York: Rowan and Littlefield.

Cook, S., and L. Binford. 1990. *Obliging Need: Rural Petty Industry in Mexican Capitalism.* Austin: University of Texas Press.

DeWalt, B. R., M. W. Rees, and A. D. Murphy. 1994. *The End of Agrarian Reform in Mexico: Past Lessons, Future Prospects.* San Francisco: Center for U.S.-Mexican Studies, University of California.

Golden, Charles. 2005. "Where Does Memory Reside and Why Isn't It History?" *AAA* 107 (2): 270–74.

Gramsci, Antonio. 1991. *Prison Notebooks*. Trans. Joseph A. Buttigieg. New York: Columbia University Press.

Gupta, Akhil, and James Ferguson. 1992. "Beyond 'Culture': Space, Identity, and the Politics of Difference." In *Cultural Anthropology* 7(1): 6–23.

——— (eds.). 1997. *Anthropological Locations: Boundaries and Grounds of a Field Science*. Berkeley: University of California Press.

Harker, Richard, Cheleen Mahar, and Chris Wilkes (eds.). 1990. *The Practice of Theory: An Introduction to the Work of Pierre Bourdieu*. London: Macmillan, and New York: St. Martin's Press.

Higgins, Michael. 1972. "'Somos gente humilde': Ethnography of a Poor Urban Colonia in Oaxaca, Mexico." Ph.D. ms. from the University of Illinois.

———. 1974. *Somos gente humilde: Etnografía de una colonia pobre, Oaxaca, Mexico*. Mexico City: Instituto Nacional Indigenista.

Hirabayashi, Lane. 1993. *Cultural Capital: Mountain Zapotec Migrant Associations in Mexico City*. Tucson: University of Arizona Press.

———. 1994. "Mountain Zapotec Migrants and Forms of Capital." In *PoLAR* 17(2): 105–16.

———. 1997. "The Politicization of Regional Identity Among Mountain Zapotec Migrants in Mexico City." In *Migrants, Regional Identities and Latin American Cities*, ed. T. Altamirano and Lane Hirabayashi. Society For Latin American Anthropology 13: 49–66.

Jameson, Fredric. 1998. *The Cultural Turn: Selected Writings on the Postmodern, 1983–1998*. London and New York: Verso.

Kearney, Michael. 1995 "The Local and the Global: The Anthropology of Globalization and Transnationalism". *Annual Review of Anthropology* 24: 547–65.

Keyes, Charles F. 2002. "Weber and Anthropology." In *Annual Review of Anthropology* 31: 233–55.

Leeds, Anthony. 1969. "The Concept of the Culture of Poverty: Conceptual, Logical and Empirical Problems, with Perspectives from Brazil and Peru." In *The Culture of Poverty: A Critique*, ed. E. Leacock. New York: Simon and Schuster.

———. 1971. "The Significant Variables Determining the Character of Squatter Settlements." In *América Latina* 2(93): 44–86.

Lewis, Oscar. 1952. "Urbanization Without Breakdown: A Case Study." In *Scientific Monthly* 75: 31–41.

———. 1959. *Children of Sánchez: Autobiography of a Mexican Family*. New York: Vintage Books.

Lomnitz, Claudio. 1994. "Decadence in Times of Globalization." In *Cultural Anthropology* 9(2): 255–67.

Mahar, Cheleen. 1987. "The Strategy of Urban Life." Unpublished dissertation, Massey University, New Zealand.

———. 1990. "Pierre Bourdieu: The Intellectual Project." In *An Introduction to the Work of Pierre Bourdieu: The Practice of Theory*. London: Macmillan Press, and New York: St. Martin's Press.

———. 1992. "An Exercise in Practice: Studying Migrants in Latin American Squatter

Settlements." *Urban Anthropology and Studies of Cultural Systems and World Economic Development* 21(3): 275–309.

———. 2000. "From Urban Migrant to Urban Citizen." *Urban Anthropology and Studies of Cultural Systems and World Economic Development* 29 (3): 359–402.

Mahar, Cheleen, and Christopher Wilkes. 2004. "Pierre Bourdieu." In *Contemporary Critical Theorists: From Lacan to Said*, ed. Jon Simons. Edinburgh: Edinburgh University Press.

Mangin, William. 1967. "Latin American Squatter Settlements: A Problem and a Solution." *Latin American Research Review* 2(3): 75.

Mead, Margaret. 1959. *Ruth Benedict, 1887–1948: An Anthropologist at Work*. Boston: Houghton Mifflin.

Murphy, Arthur. 1983. "The Economic Groups of Oaxaca". In *Somos Tocayos: The Anthropology of Urbanism and Poverty*, ed. Michael Higgins. Lanham, Md.: University Press of America.

Murphy, Arthur, and Alex Stepick. 1991. *Social Inequality in Oaxaca: A History Of Resistance and Change*. Philadelphia: Temple University Press.

Nash, June C. 2007. *Practicing Ethnography in a Globalizing World: An Anthropological Odyssey*. London: AltaMira Press.

Paddock, John. 1966. *Ancient Oaxaca*. Stanford, Calif.: Stanford University Press.

Perlman, Janice. 1976. *The Myth of Marginality: Urban Poverty and Politics in Rio de Janeiro*. Berkeley: University of California Press.

Rees, Martha, Arthur Murphy, Earl Morris, and Mary Winter. 1991. "Migrants to and in Oaxaca City." *Urban Anthropology* 20(1): 15–30.

Rosaldo, Renato. 1994. "From Cultural Citizenship and Educational Democracy." In *Cultural Anthropology* 9(3): 402–11.

Rouse, Roger. 1991. "Mexican Migration and the Social Space of Postmodernism." In *Diaspora* 1(1): 8–23.

———. 1992. "Making Sense of Settlement: Class Transformation, Cultural Struggle, and Transnationalism among Mexican Migrants in the United States." In *Towards a Transnational Perspective on Migration: Race, Class, Ethnicity, and Nationalism Reconsidered*, ed. Ninna Glick Schiller and Cristina Szanton-Blanc. Annals of the New York Academy of Sciences 645: 25–52.

Rubel, Arthur, C. W. O'Neill, and R. Collado-Ardon. 1991. *Susto: A Folk Illness*. Berkeley: University of California Press.

Scott, Robert E. (ed.). 1973. *Latin American Modernization Problems: Case Studies in the Crisis of Change*. Urbana: University of Illinois.

Schultz, William Todd (ed.). 2005. *Handbook of Psychobiography*. Oxford: Oxford University Press.

Selby, Henry. 1991. Foreword to *Social Inequality in Oaxaca: A History Of Resistance and Change*, by Arthur Murphy and Alex Stepick. Philadelphia: Temple University Press.

Stephen, Lynn. 1991. *Zapotec Women*. Austin: University of Texas Press.

Turner, John. 1991. *Housing By People: Towards Autonomy in Building Environments*. Reprinted. London: Marion Boyars Publishers.

Uchitelle, Louis. 2007. "Age of Riches: The Richest of the Rich, Proud of a Gilded Age." *New York Times* Web site, July 15.

Valentine, Charles. 1968. *Culture and Poverty: Critique and Counter-Proposals.* Chicago: University of Chicago Press.

Wacquant, Loic. 1999. "America as Social Dystopia." In *The Weight of the World,* by Pierre Bourdieu et al. Stanford, Calif.: Stanford University Press.

Wallis, Jim. 2006. *God's Politics: Why The Right Gets It Wrong and the Left Doesn't Get It.* New York: HarperCollins.

Weber, Max. 1958 [1930]. *The Protestant Ethic and the Spirit of Capitalism.* Trans. T. Parsons. New York: Scribner's Sons.

———. 2004. "Science as a Vocation." In *The Vocation Lectures.* Indianapolis: Hackett Publishing.

Wolf, Eric. 1959. *Sons of the Shaking Earth: The People of Mexico and Guatemala— Their Land, History, and Culture.* Chicago: University of Chicago Press.

Note: Italic page numbers refer to figures.